POEMS OF GWE

BORDER VOICES:

POEMS OF GWENT AND MONMOUTHSHIRE

Edited with an Introduction and Notes by
GERAINT EIRUG DAVIES

First Impression—1999

ISBN 1 85902 567 6

This book is published with the support of the
Arts Council of Wales.

Printed in Wales at
Gomer Press, Llandysul, Ceredigion

I GOFIO'N DDIOLCHGAR AM
DYFNALLT MORGAN
(1917-1994)

CONTENTS

ABERGAVENNY AND THE BLACK MOUNTAINS

THE RIVER USK
AND THE PASTORAL HEART OF GWENT

MONMOUTH AND THE WYE VALLEY

THE SEVERN

MISCELLANEOUS

INTRODUCTION

This is an anthology of Gwent and Monmouthshire poems. Such an enterprise has not been attempted since Lawrence Hockey's *Monmouthshire Poetry* appeared fifty years ago in 1949. Since that date the literary past has been re-evaluated and a new generation of younger poets has also emerged. This anthology pays due regard to the considerable achievements of poets writing in or about Gwent or Monmouthshire in the last fifty years.

Hockey's collection was based on the work of some thirty-three poets, of whom fourteen are represented in this anthology. Hockey's anthology included English translations of Welsh poems by Dafydd ap Gwilym and Islwyn: I have preferred to present the Welsh language poets of Gwent in their original language with English translations alongside the Welsh. A biographical section on the poets helps to establish the local connection for the reader and notes to the poems are also included.

An explanation of the criteria underlying the choice of poems is in order. My interpretation of Gwent and Monmouthshire is a broad one, encompassing not only poets born or living or working in the county, but also 'visitors' who have written about the area. It has been well observed that whatever our place it has been visited by the stranger.

There is a variety about the collection with poets from the past appearing alongside those writing today. Thus Thomas Churchyard, Thomas Vaughan, Robert Bloomfield, Wordsworth, Walter Savage Landor, Tennyson and Edward Thomas appear, as well as Sam Adams, Alison Bielski, Gillian Clarke, Catherine Fisher and Christopher Meredith. Some of the poems have not hitherto been published; some are well-known and frequently anthologised. The familiar work gains a certain freshness from a new context, such as this anthology affords. The popular ballad of today and the cherished classic are included: the reader may find here both Harri Webb's 'The Stars of Mexico' and Wordsworth's 'Lines Written a Few Miles above Tintern Abbey'.

Of the eighteen Welsh-language poets represented, eleven were either born or spent some considerable time in the county. The early poets, sometimes somewhat loosely labelled bards of the gentry – Dafydd ap Gwilym, Lewys Glyn Cothi, Guto'r Glyn, Dafydd Llwyd and Dafydd Benwyn – sang in praise of their Gwent patrons. The eighteenth century is represented by a little-known hymn by Edmund Williams and Ieuan Brydydd Hir's haunting elegiac verses on the Hall of Ifor the Generous, Dafydd ap Gwilym's fourteenth-century patron. In terms of output the nineteenth century marks something of a pinnacle of achievement for Gwent poetry in Welsh. Islwyn is often regarded as the greatest Welsh-language poet of his century. I trust moreover that something of the energy of the nineteenth century has been conveyed by the inclusion of such minor poets as Ioan Emlyn, Gwentwyson and Eiddil Gwent, all prominent members of Cymreigyddion y Fenni, one of the most famous Welsh societies of the day. Few are aware that Evan James who wrote the words of the Welsh national anthem in 1856 lived at one period of his life in Argoed in the parish of Bedwellty. Only four Welsh-language poets are included from the twentieth century – Crwys, W.J.Gruffydd, Trefin and Idris Davies. Idris Davies is, of course, better known as an English poet but one of his Welsh-language poems is represented here, just as one of Islwyn's English-language lyrics is also included.

I have been encouraged to include the Welsh-language poets in their original language by the renewed interest in the Welsh cultural inheritance of Gwent. Occasionally, as in Dafydd ap Gwilym's poem, I have made use of published translations. Dyfnallt Morgan's translation of Guto'r Glyn and John Gwilym Jones's translation of Dafydd Llwyd were undertaken specifically for this anthology and will go far to dispel Coleridge's idea of the 'untranslateableness' of poetry. Most of the remaining translations, for what they are worth, are mine. In all cases the original text remains the primary one: the translations (mostly literal) are simply an attempt at making the Welsh past available to English speakers.

The two most famous poets of Gwent are W.H.Davies, the tramp poet, and Idris Davies, whose work represented for

T.S.Eliot 'the best poetic document . . . about a particular epoch in a particular place'. These two are of course featured in this anthology. Lawrence Hockey's collection included far more poems by W.H.Davies than by Idris Davies. My anthology reflects current poetic taste in reversing that trend: there are fifteen poems by Idris Davies; five by W .H. Davies. The comparatively unknown Myfanwy Haycock – at her best an accomplished lyricist – is also extensively represented here. Some of the poets are essentially local authors, most effective when they write about a particular locality: Edward Davies and Ivor Waters are primarily Chepstow poets, recreating for the reader a lively sense of the town in the eighteenth and twentieth centuries respectively.

The variety of this collection has been stressed yet the anthology has a strong unity in its concern with what I like to call 'the Gwent experience'. The anthology reflects the history, geography and culture of Gwent in highlighting the complex character of this fascinating border county with its manifold contradictions and contrasts. Such oppositions as Wales/England, Welsh/English, Gwent/Monmouthshire, rural/industrial occur naturally in Gwent and are surely to be regarded as enriching in their very complexity. Monmouthshire is included in the title of this anthology, since most of the poets represented here wrote as Monmouthshire poets between 1536 and 1974. The original Monmouthshire, let us remind ourselves, was formed in 1536 following the Act of Union between England and Wales. Before 1536, Gwent along with Gwynllwg was a *cantref* of Morgannwg. With local government organisation in 1974, Monmouthshire became integrated into the new county of Gwent in a reversion to the name which had originally applied to the district enclosed by the rivers Usk, Wye, Monnow and the sea. In April 1996 the emergence of the new unitary authorities brought about the disappearance of Gwent and a renewal of Monmouthshire, albeit on a much smaller scale. This anthology may serve therefore as an appropriate poetic tribute to both Gwent and Monmouthshire, as they have existed for many centuries.

The earlier references to the rivers remind one, above all, of the county's magnificent landscape which remains, whether we refer to Gwent or Monmouthshire. We are never far away from a glimpse of this landscape in this anthology. It is no coincidence that one of the greatest landscape poems in the English language, Wordsworth's 'Lines Written a Few Miles above Tintern Abbey', was inspired by a Monmouthshire scene. Perhaps John Tripp's lines from his poem 'The Elders', which though not included here, half echo Wordsworth and sum up the underlying sentiment of this anthology:

> For who loves not his own patch
>   of plundered soil, learns nothing of pity
>   for all men.

Since this anthology is rooted in a sense of place, it seems appropriate to attempt a geographical arrangement for the poems. I begin my journey in the industrial valleys of Gwent which dominate the anthology much as they have done in the real-life experience of the county. Then there is a sequence of poems based on Abergavenny and the Black Mountains. This section is followed by poems on the River Usk and the Pastoral Heart of Gwent. From Monmouth and the Wye Valley I travel to the Severn and a final section comprises those poems which deal either with Gwent or Monmouthshire as a whole or with themes that have no direct link with a specific place. The reader will forgive my occasional sortie into Breconshire and Herefordshire. Blame those magical rivers – the Usk and the Monnow – for taking me on an occasional journey upstream to places beyond the strict boundaries of Gwent.

GERAINT EIRUG DAVIES
Caerleon

THE WESTERN VALLEYS

I WAS BORN IN RHYMNEY
(Extract)

I was born in Rhymney
To a miner and his wife –
On a January morning
I was pulled into this Life.

Among Anglicans and Baptists
And Methodists I grew,
And my childhood had to chew and chance
The creeds of such a crew.

I went to church and chapel
Ere I could understand
That Apollo rules the heavens
And Mammon rules the land.

And I woke on many mornings
In a little oblong room,
And saw the frown of Spurgeon:
"Beware, my boy, of doom."

And there was the family Bible
Beneath a vase of flowers,
With pictures of the Holy Land
That enchanted me for hours.

And there was my Uncle Edward,
Solemn and stern and grey,
A Calvinistic Methodist
Who made me kneel and pray.

He would carry me on his shoulders
When I was six or seven
And tell me of the golden days
When chariots flew to heaven.

He was furious against Pharaoh
And scornful about Eve,
But his pathos about Joseph
Could always make me grieve.

He knew the tribes and customs
And the apt geography
Of Jerusalem and Jericho
And the hills of Galilee.

And Moses was his hero
And Jehovah was his God.
And his stories were as magical
As Aaron's magic rod.

But sometimes from the Bible
He would turn to politics
And tell of Gladstone's glory
And Disraeli's little tricks.

But even William Ewart Gladstone
Of beloved memory
Would fade and be forgotten
When it came to D.L.G.

The little Celt from Criccieth,
The Liberal on fire,
He was the modern Merlin
And Moses and Isaiah!

The ghost of Uncle Edward
In a solemn bowler hat,
Does it haunt the plains of Moab
Or the slopes of Ararat?

Or lurks it in the Gateway,
Where Peter holds the key,
To welcome on the harp strings
The ghost of D.L.G.?

I lost my native language
For the one the Saxon spake
By going to school by order
For education's sake.

I learnt the use of decimals,
And where to place the dot,
Four or five lines from Shakespeare
And twelve from Walter Scott.

I learnt a little grammar,
And some geography,
Was frightened of perspective,
And detested poetry.

In a land of narrow valleys,
And solemn Sabbath Days,
And collieries and choirs,
I learnt my people's ways.

I looked on local deacons
With not a little awe,
I waved a penny Union Jack
When Asquith went to war.

I pinned my faith in Kitchener
And later in Haig and Foch,
And pitied little Belgium
And cursed the bloody Boche.

We warred along the hillsides
And volleyed sticks and stones,
And sometimes smashed the windows
Of Mrs Hughes and Jones.

We stood in queues for apples,
For paraffin, and jam,
And were told to spit on Lenin,
And honour Uncle Sam.

But often in the evenings
When all the stars were out
We played beneath the lamp-post
And did not stop to doubt

That the world was made for children
Early on Christmas Day
By a jolly old whiskered Josser
In a mansion far away.

And there were the hours for Chaplin,
Pearl White, and Buffalo Bill,
And the hours for nests and whinberries
High on the summer hill.

And O the hour of lilac
And a leopard in the sky,
And the heart of childhood singing
A song that cannot die!

I learnt of Saul and Jesus
In the little Sunday School,
And later learnt to muse and doubt
By some lonely mountain pool.

I saw that creeds could comfort
And hypocrisy console
But in my blood were battles
No Bible could control.

And I praised the unknown Artist
Of crag and fern and stream
For the sunshine on the mountains
And the wonder of a dream.

On one February morning,
Unwillingly I went
To crawl in moleskin trousers
Beneath the rocks of Gwent.

And a chubby little collier
Grew fat on sweat and dust,
And listened to heated arguments
On God and Marx and lust.

For seven years among the colliers
I learnt to laugh and curse,
When times were fairly prosperous
And when they were ten times worse.

And I loved and loved the mountains
Against the cloudy sky,
The sidings, and the slag-heaps
That sometimes hurt the eye.

MacDonald was my hero,
The man who seemed inspired,
The leader with a vision,
Whose soul could not be hired!

I quoted from his speeches
In the coalface to my friends –
But I lived to see him selling
Great dreams for little ends.

And there were strikes and lock-outs
And meetings in the Square,
When Cook and Smith and Bevan
Electrified the air.

But the greatest of our battles
We lost in '26
Through treachery and lying,
And Baldwin's box of tricks.

I began to read from Shelley
In afternoons in May,
And to muse upon the misery
Of unemployment pay.

I stood in queues for hours
Outside the drab Exchange,
With my hands deep in my pockets
In a suit I could not change.

I stood before Tribunals
And smothered all my pride,
And bowed to my inferiors,
And raged with my soul outside.

And I walked my native hillsides
In sunshine and in rain,
And learnt the poet's language
To ease me of my pain.

With Wordsworth and with Shelley
I scribbled out my dreams,
Sometimes among the slag-heaps,
Sometimes by mountain streams.

O I shook hands with Shelley
Among the moonlit fern,
And he smiled, and slowly pointed
To the heart that would not burn.

And I discovered Milton
In a shabby little room
Where I spent six summer evenings
In most luxurious gloom.

I met Macbeth and Lear,
And Falstaff full of wine,
And I went one day to Stratford
To tread on ground divine.

And I toiled through dismal evenings
With algebraical signs,
With Euclid and Pythagoras
And all their points and lines.

Sometimes there came triumph
But sometimes came despair,
And I would fling all books aside
And drink the midnight air.

And there were dark and bitter mornings
When the streets like coffins lay
Between the winter mountains,
Long and bleak and grey.

But season followed season
And beauty never died
And there were days and hours
Of hope and faith and pride.

In springtime I went roaming
Along the Severn Sea,
Rejoicing in the tempest
And its savage ecstasy.

And there were summer evenings
By Taf, and Usk, and Wye,
When the land was bright with colour
Beneath a quiet sky.

But always home to Rhymney
From wandering I came,
Back to the long and lonely
Self-tuition game,

Back to Euclid's problems,
And algebraical signs,
And the routes of trade and commerce,
And Caesar's battle lines,

Back to the lonely evenings
Of triumph and despair
In a little room in Rhymney
With a hint of mountain air.

O days I shall remember
Until I drop and die! —
Youth's bitter sweet progression
Beneath a Rhymney sky.

Idris Davies

MY SONG

Today and tomorrow and the day after that
My song is of Rhymney, and the rose, and the rat,
And the wonder of science, and the magic of art,
And the night and the morning of the sensitive heart.

Idris Davies

CWMSYFIOG

How long ago, no one can tell,
Some Welshman named you Strawberry Dell,
But now, by your polluted stream,
I see nor strawberries nor cream.

Idris Davies

HEN WLAD FY NHADAU

Mae hen wlad fy nhadau yn annwyl i mi,
Gwlad beirdd a chantorion, enwogion o fri;
Ei gwrol ryfelwyr, gwladgarwyr tra mad,
Dros ryddid collasant eu gwaed.

Cytgan
Gwlad! Gwlad! pleidiol wyf i'm Gwlad;
Tra mor yn fur i'r bur hoff bau,
O, bydded i'r heniaith barhau!

Hen Gymru fynyddig, paradwys y bardd,
Pob dyffryn, pob clogwyn i'm golwg sydd hardd;
Trwy deimlad gwladgarol mor swynol yw si
Ei nentydd, afonydd i mi.

Os treisiodd y gelyn fy ngwlad dan ei droed,
Mae heniaith y Cymry mor fyw ag erioed;
Ni luddiwyd yr awen gan erchylllaw brad,
Na thelyn berseiniol fy ngwlad.

Evan James

LAND OF MY FATHERS

The land of my fathers, the land of my choice,
The land in which poets and minstrels rejoice;
The land whose stern warriors were true to the core,
While bleeding for freedom of yore.

Chorus
Wales! Wales! favourite land of Wales!
While sea her wall, may naught befall
To mar the old language of Wales!

Old Cambria of mountains, the Eden of bards,
Each hill and each valley excite my regards,
To the ears of her patriots how charming still seems
The music that flows in her streams.

My country, though crushed by a hostile array,
The language of Cambria survives to this day;
The muse has eluded the traitors' foul knives,
The harp of my country survives.

Translated by Eben Fardd

THE SACRED ROAD

They walked this road in seasons past
When all the skies were overcast,
They breathed defiance as they went
Along these troubled hills of Gwent.

They talked of justice as they strode
Along this crooked mountain road,
And dared the little lords of Hell
So that the future should be well.

Because they did not count the cost
But battled on when all seemed lost,
This empty ragged road shall be
Always a sacred road to me.

                                        Idris Davies

MONMOUTHSHIRE

In Parliament they ponder
   On Monmouth's pedigree;
Or is she Welsh or English
   In the page of history?
But those who know her people
   Among the smoking vales
Proclaim with pride that they were born
   In Monmouthshire, Wales.

In Monmouth or Glamorgan,
   You doubt not where you are,
Your fate is fixed for good or bad
   Beneath a Celtic star;
And they who will are welcome
   To fill their skulls with tales,
But my address is Rhymney,
   In Monmouthshire, Wales.

Idris Davies

IN THE PLACES OF MY BOYHOOD

In the places of my boyhood
   The pit-wheels turn no more,
Nor any furnace lightens
   The midnight as of yore.

The slopes of slag and cinder
   Are sulking in the rain,
And in derelict valleys
   The hope of youth is slain.

And yet I love to wander
   The early ways I went,
And watch from doors and bridges
   The hills and skies of Gwent.

Though blighted be the valleys
   Where man meets man with pain,
The things my boyhood cherished
   Stand firm, and shall remain.

Idris Davies

THE NORTHERN SLOPES

The northern slopes are clouded
   And Rhymney streets are wet,
The winds sweep down from the mountains
   And night has cast her net.

The ghosts of a thousand miners
   Walk back to the streets again,
And the winds wail in the darkness,
   And Rhymney sighs in the rain.

Idris Davies

HIGH SUMMER ON THE MOUNTAINS

High summer on the mountains
And on the clover leas,
And on the local sidings,
And on the rhubarb leaves.

Brass bands in all the valleys
Blaring defiant tunes,
Crowds, acclaiming carnival,
Prize pigs and wooden spoons.

Dust on shabby hedgerows
Behind the colliery wall,
Dust on rail and girder
And tram and prop and all.

High summer on the slag heaps
And on polluted streams,
And old men in the morning
Telling the town their dreams.

Idris Davies

IN THE DUSK

When the mountains are grey in the evening
    And cool are the winds from the west
And the lights in the valleys are twinkling
    And the birds and the beasts go to rest,
I hear the strange echoes of armies
    That glittered and conquered of old,
That marched to the beat of the ages
    And lay down to sleep in the mould.

And I dream of the prince and the peasant
    Who died for Glamorgan and Gwent,
And the Norman who scorned the Silurian
    And ravaged the way that he went,
And the blood on the walls and the arches,
    And the sweat of the toilers untold
Who toiled to the beat of the ages
    And lay down to sleep in the mould.

Idris Davies

THE CURLEWS OF BLAEN RHYMNI

The curlews of Blaen Rhymni are calling in the night
And all the hills are magical because the moon is bright,
And I walk alone, and listen, along the mountain way
To curlew calling curlew in hollows far away.

And the crying of the curlew makes more sad and strange
    and fair
The moon above the moorland and the clear midnight air,
And the mountain breeze is laden with some echoes that
    must be
The echoes of a music beyond humanity.

And curlew calls to curlew, and I remember as I go
The merrier sounds and echoes out of seasons long ago,
When the nights were full of laughter and all the days were
    bright
And the hearts too young to listen to the curlew in the
    night.

Idris Davies

O WHAT CAN YOU GIVE ME?

O what can you give me?
Say the sad bells of Rhymney.

Is there hope for the future?
Cry the brown bells of Merthyr.

Who made the mineowner?
Say the black bells of Rhondda.

And who robbed the miner?
Cry the grim bells of Blaina.

They will plunder willy-nilly,
Say the bells of Caerphilly.

They have fangs, they have teeth!
Shout the bells of Neath.

To the south, things are sullen,
Say the pink bells of Brecon.

Even God is uneasy,
Say the moist bells of Swansea.

Put the vandals in court!
Cry the bells of Newport.

And would be well if – if- if –
Say the green bells of Cardiff.

Why so worried, sisters, why?
Sing the silver bells of Wye.

Idris Davies

CWM RHYMNI

Ar lannau Afon Rhymni
Mi grwydrais lawer tro
Pan nad oedd hwyl i ganu
Ym mwg y pyllau glo.

Ar lethrau llwyd Cwm Rhymni
Yn oriau'r gwynt a'r glaw,
Trist oeddwn yn breuddwydio
Am ryw binaclau draw.

Pinaclau'r oesoedd euraidd
Tu hwnt i'r dydd a'r nos,
Breuddwydion ffôl y galon
A'u gwreiddiau yn y rhos.

Ond 'nawr, ple bynnag crwydraf,
Mae miwsig yn fy ngho'
Am fachgen yn breuddwydio
Ym mwg y pyllau glo.

Idris Davies

RHYMNEY VALLEY

On the banks of the River Rhymney
I wandered many a time,
When I lacked inspiration to sing
In the smoke of the coal mines.

On the grey slopes of the Rhymney Valley,
In hours of wind and rain,
I was sad, dreaming
Of some distant pinnacles.

The pinnacles of some golden age
Beyond day and night,
The foolish dreams of the heart
With their roots in the moors.

But now, whenever I wander,
There is music in my memories
Of a boy, dreaming
In the smoke of the coal mines.

Translated by the Editor

MINER

There are countless tons of rock above his head,
And gases wait in secret corners for a spark;
And his lamp shows dimly in the dust.
His leather belt is warm and moist with sweat,
And he crouches against the hanging coal,
And the pick swings to and fro,
And many beads of salty sweat play about his lips
And trickle down the blackened skin
To the hairy tangle on his chest.
The rats squeak and scamper among the unused props,
And the fungus waxes strong.

Idris Davies

A STAR IN THE EAST

When Christmastide to Rhymney came
    And I was six or seven
I thought the stars in the eastern sky
    Were the brightest stars of heaven.

I chose the star that glittered most
    To the east of Rhymney town
To be the star above the byre
    Where Mary's babe lay down.

And nineteen hundred years would meet
    Beneath a magic light,
And Rhymney share with Bethlehem
    A star on Christmas night.

Idris Davies

IN MEMORY OF IDRIS DAVIES
(for Glyn Jones)

He was short and sturdy, one of dim Picton's Silurians –
dark, tough, stocky, thick-necked and durable,
bantam of a race that went down before the blond Celts,
then packed the pits and Big Seats and choirs and scrums.
When you saw him in a drizzle on the Capitol steps
he wore a cloth cap, wool muffler, gloves and brown mac
with old wire specs askew, mended on wet-look solder,
one pebble-lens flattened tight to the eyeball.
He held his collier's Woodbine in the cup of his wounded
    hand,
easy and serene, without sulk or boiling mouth.

Rhymney and poverty made him. He was haunted to the
    very end
by the skull of want and the furious gospel
lashed from the radical pulpits. Green dawns of childhood
by the river and black alp, dust-hung summer afternoons
among nettles in the pityard with the lost ragged boys
led him and them to the customary crawl
under the earth, along the seams of Gwent,
thin layer of grime washed off into the evening tub.
Then the long lonely track to shape himself,
the bitter chronicle beginning to itch inside his mind.

Out of such parched soil, such pitiless rock
his harsh plant grew. No document was ever carved before
from this slab of ferocity and love –
a wept lament for all those diggers in the dark
and their broken kin, abandoned in the tunnels of the south,
a testament of disgust drilled at the core of wrong.
He never served an image of moonlit brooks
or salmon-running streams, or blue remembered hills.

His was a bedded landscape of human figures
bent but proud before a random wind.

Memory must have plagued him like a pox
as his exiled heart was shuttled about England,
as honesty tested his acceptance
through the soft quilted ease of Bohemia.
In the staff-rooms of mouldering schools,
what remark could have triggered a vision
that shot him straight back to his bleakest ridge?
In those gay nights of bellowing talk,
did the turnkey suddenly slide in his greasy coat
to show him the ramshackle beauty of Wales?

Stripped, bare, stark and pure the lyrics come,
hard and lovely as the place that formed him,
true as the tribute to his ravaged land.
His goodness seeps down the years to remind us
of faith to be kept in the ruins. His last limp
over the mountain road, his suit hung loose on the frail
    bones,
will take him south again to the buttercup fields,
to the dream in the vale when he was young.
Your sad bells of Rhymney ring sweet and clear, Idris,
and the pigeons are homing. They are coming home.

John Tripp

HOMAGE TO ANEURIN BEVAN

The last time the silver cascaded for me
was at Brentford, of all places. He walked
between two awed local agents
who revelled in short glory
with this paramount trapper of hypocrites,
this Welsh word-weaver famed for his coup de grâce.

No one knew then, it was near the end,
he was sick even then as we heard
him lunge at the ones who could never grasp
his gospel, at the clever who could handle
brilliance for a minute in the chamber
when he stayed on facts,
but were lost when he purred in the venom,
whipped when he launched the tirades.

The slight lisp was still there as he thundered,
drumming up compassion for the poor, still
boxing with the governors to take drabness
out of ill-favoured lives,
lifting his hand as if to snuff out a candle,
shocking us again with the unmatched wit,
the logic clear as glass.

It is easy to be brave in company, linking hands,
but this one was out on the ramparts, night after night,
alone. And when he disappeared,
a portcullis slammed down,
leaving the captain of archers outside.

John Tripp

A VOICE IN THE WIND

The wind blows in old memories like dead leaves,
Inconsequential, tumbling, then one sticks
Tapping, tapping, impossible to dislodge,
Places, names, none of them somehow quite
The expected visitor. They've been there all the time
Whirling about in the dark, now they won't go,
Tapping, tapping, names, memories.
The wind in my roof tonight blows in from the Waun Pond,
High common above three valleys crammed
With small houses and huge wrongs, the air
Brisk, the northern crop of the coal-measures,
Abrupt frontier between slagheaps and rough pasture.
That's where I saw you, heard you, shook your hand.
Our paths touched an instant, that was all.
You stood on the back of a lorry, spoke to a crowd
Of perhaps a thousand, a politician in a smart suit,
Master of oratory, at home, confident, in command,
The world was listening. Unconsciously I noted
Your back was turned to the hills, you gestured
Always to the valley below. You spoke of a dream,
Summoning your people – yes, they were your people,
Yours, and you were their leader, you held them
In the hollow of your hand – to build anew
Where the old tyrants had cheated and despoiled.
The crowd was silent. It could have been a scene
Anytime in our history, the chieftain aloft
And the host mustered to follow.

                    Already though
It was something of a sentimental pilgrimage,
The spot chosen because here in the starving years
The gaunt contigents had converged from Rhymni,
Tredegar, Ebbw Vale, the Valleys of the Shadow,
To seek a dawn, and even on that day
Of sunshine and solidarity, there was somehow
The breath of premonition that all too soon
There would be no more such meetings, nor no man
Like this one to inspire them, and the people
Would have found other places to go, the Waun Pond
As unregarded as before the first forges
Flamed in Gwent. Here and there in the crowd
The older men whispered this behind their hands
And drew their belted raincoats closer around them.
But I will not begrudge you or myself the bright memory
Of Aneurin Bevan standing against the sky,
A Silurian prince, even though you lost your way.

                                        Harri Webb

MEMORIAL TO ANEURIN BEVAN

Limestone with common touch,
swept by winds whose passion burned the grass to straw
and seared the bearded bullrush.
In a magic triangle of ancient power,
standing alone among the three, on Waun-y-Pound.
Thousands stood, Dai-capped, muffled,
upturned their collars against the cold,
ears reddened by the bite and fire of his oratory.
Strong medicine for weaker men.
Looked up to him, black as the swooping jackdaw,
outlined on a white sky.
Eyes hurting, too bright for clear sight.
Left,
against the stone,
a car seat, skeletal, padding decomposed,
hunched over sheep droppings and broken bottles once full
     of gas,
where those who would not be counted
sat and watched the matted sheep and the mountain pony,
cropping and moving slowly over old tracks.

Local names, scratched deeply, keep company.
        Sian was here. Wayne was here.
        Ron and Archie. Michael. Jennie.
His flame burned out, ashes scattered,
tempered by opposing elements, a smoothing over and
forgetting.
The rock stands, unmoved,
rising above other memorials.
Old bones whitening on the hillside.

                                          Irene Thomas

CAWL

Nosy, my mother would have said,
forgetting
the comfort of the vegetable stew
round Spitalfields,
the seasoned streets that nourished her beginning.
(Into the basic stock
from the last boiling
went the ingredients fresh plucked,
the new uprootings
from Polish plains and muddy English shires.)

Nosy, she would have said, because
emerging
from that rich cheek by jowl
to suburbs where you kept a decent distance
(the plate with meat and two veg not quite touching)
required her to suppress
the natural question,
adopt a cautious reticence,
avoiding
the answer that involved your life with theirs.

Nosy, she would have said, when I,
arriving
a stranger at a Valleys station,
was seized upon,
subjected to intense interrogation:
where was I from, and where
would I be staying?
Why had I come? Describe myself –
including
my schooling, prospects, parents, hopes and fears.

Nosy, she would have said to that,
mistaking
the hunger to relate, absorb, enfold
and understand
for indefensible and shameless prying.
Had she but settled here
and dipped a sample spoon,
I can imagine her delight
in tasting
again the broth that fed her childhood years.

Questioning, while these Valley towns
were growing,
processed the elements from which they grew;
exploring and comparing and defining
hastened the cooking of a common view.
The basic stock combined
with flavours of West Wales,
and Cork and Gloucester – blending and
becoming
a bowl where isolation disappears.

Mick Morden

COAL DUST GREY
(Colliers Row)

Washing
Billowing across the bailey.
Shirts and spencers,
Combinations,
Merging into
Coal dust grey.

Turn the mangle.
Pound the dolly,
Wooden pegs dance on the line.
Sheets and blankets
Turned to middle,
Patched and washed
A coal dust grey.

Baby clothes,
Their pristine whiteness
Hanging short
On rusty lines
Cradled in the grimy breezes,
Growing into
Coal dust grey.

"Quick it's raining."
Grab the washing,
Joust the prop, wind in the line.
Make your Mam
A living clothes horse,
Saddled
With the coal dust grey.

Pit and mangle, move together,
Married in an endless motion.
Starch and blue-bag,
Pick and shovel,
Turning Love
A coal dust grey.

Irene Thomas

WASHING DAY

It's washing day in Monmouthshire;
Along the swirly-whirly streams
The celandines have lit a fire.
It seems, it seems,

That every valley is a tub,
A'foam with apple-blossom suds,
Where wind and rain and sunshine scrub
The new, fat buds

Of oaks and elms and sycamores.
With gurgles, giggles, grunts and groans
The brooks have scoured their pebbly floors
Like clean, white bones.

Half-glimpsed through tattered water-shrouds,
Across the blue, high-arching sky
Are rows and rows of puffy clouds
Hung up to dry.

Upon the hill the little house
In fine new whitewash sits and stares
Bright-eyed, like a bewildering mouse.
The hawthorn wears

A crisp new coat of green; the lane
That hops downhill and leaps the streams
Is splashed with primroses and rain.
It seems, it seems

That every valley's full of foam
Of steam and sunshine, froth and fire –
It's windy washing day at home
In Monmouthshire.

Myfanwy Haycock

SACRIFICIAL LAMBS

I first heard the black ones crying
and learned of their fleecing,
as I wet-breathed
through the warmth of their fibres.

They cropped the tip on Gantre,
until cold snaps worried,
and drove them to forage in Colliers Row,
pawing buckets until they spilled,
grazing ice with clinker and ash.
In the night came the crack of horn on wood
as they rammed shored-up gates,
and shouldered into frozen gardens,
gnawing at stunted stalks and sprouts
solid as a sinker's knuckles.

They sheltered in gulleys
between the houses,
and dry coughed the darkness away.

Stiff and ravenous,
they matted outside half doors,
heading for curled peelings
and outside leaves.

In spite of meagre staple,
came lambs, born on Gantre shale,
and we heard them bleating
for lost mothers and for milk,
and there was no shepherd,
except for the counting and the killing.

In summer,
ewes panted under patchy winter coats,
scrubbed skin raw
and left woollen shreds
hanging on black tar wires.

The old ones defended
against dogs who threatened
and losers made carrion for crows.
Jack-daws,
loud mouthed keepers of the pecking order,
spread a shivering pall, bruise-black
over common branding and seared flesh.
A few grey hairs remained,
and a scattering of teeth
worn down with grinding.

They were poor man's meat
and on the chopping block
their heads split
with tempered blade and pounder,
half-brained with steel.
Tongues stilled in aspic.

Irene Thomas

SHEEP

This one, you guess, looking at me, is the leader.
His stare is not a challenge. Nothing. Just a stare.
And the way the others clutter behind him in the wagon.
This, you think, is some photo of an old war. Clothes
ragged, cropped heads, children dazed calling for food,
all the thin legs merded with crammed travel
and eyes indifferent with many deaths.
The eyes, you think, must haunt the guards at compound gate
hinting of seeing through all things.
Perhaps you feel yourself melt a little, feel naked
when I look at you.

We have been a rich vein for you,
for your languages and rites.
Your god was one of us, you say
yet also our crooked captor, caring for us
clinical with our surgery
his outstretched manpicture your mangod picture.
We have been: The Lost, The Wanderers, The Sufferers.
You have set us on high and taken our flesh.
This is no injustice. Only irony.

Sitting with your car door pushed open in the afternoon
one foot on the earth
tea in the flask, a map in the glovebox
you can look around the country where we are kept
and feel no wryness –
feel warmed even, in the dozing lanes
hate the smoke and motorways you came out of
before you turn back.
But you catch my eye a moment on the passing wagon.
Reflected there you see all the rolling vale
your fallen eden unfolded and become
a heaving green belsen.

Christopher Meredith

CEFN GOLAU IN SNOW

Some places give almost nothing.
Stare hard and you can almost see
horizons where off-white meets off-white.
The sky can be a wash of greys
and when the wash thins
the sun can rub a pale disc
on a frozen screen.
Dwarf trees can crab like script
against the snow.
Far off, broken places in the ground
make punctuation where
there are no words.

Yet turn an invisible corner on the hill
and down there, estates and towns
blot through in smirched insistent chains.
Clouds shred like battlesmoke.
Colour abrading the eye with its grit
is the houses clinging to the slush lanes,
heaped cars rusting in a compound.

Christopher Meredith

TAKING MY MOTHER TO TROED

We saunter along both the rows
And at each door she names a ghost,
The family history and how
They died, or moved, or why they stayed.
Rob Roberts her father, Auntie Ada,
Pen Rogers, George Wimblett like a
Daicapped christ heaving firewood,
Mason's Farm, The Woods, New Pits.
Naming of the haunts and haunters
Somehow fixes things, though names
Like colours come loose in the dark.

On top row a bus turns, empty.
From grass erupting through the tar,
The burnt-out school, the breezeblocked doors,
She looks up to the breaking hill.
"Oh good god, o' course it've moved."
She wonders at the few who've stayed,
Says she would not go back to this. So
Sadness would be affectation
Making us the passing tourists
Eager to be sentimental
About sheepshit, empty buildings.

Christopher Meredith

IN EBENEZER CHURCHYARD, SIRHOWY

On this grey smear of a weak day
the rasp of a forced gate
explodes impossibly.
Rubbish cast by the wall
blares in the eyes.
In winter light, you think,
it should all break and fade.
Drizzle smudges all the edges
makes eyes thirst for colour
soaks without sensation
makes feet soundless
the air sodden bland and comfortless.
In the grey nothing edges of graves
butt pallidly into vision, geometry
scraped on the rain.

There is no tradition to say this.
Here is no stone tower to crutch
a wrong church nor yew to undermine
with his older root the shallow ruler. Only
a shanty-town of leaning slabs
picked over with a fuss of letters
curled to remember the sweep of a nib.
There quench the eye.
Jane Pryce diweddar o Swydd Feirionydd
dead with her baby and others respectable
only their trades in English
all quietly rubbing to nothing on the air.

The children from the flats
have gone home on their bikes
taken the colour with them
except by the wall on the beaten grass
the busted plastic bag leaks cellophane

and printed cardboard darkening with wet
but clear enough for eyes to seize
to drink from greedily
in a bare place in the rain blur.

So these are the ones who walked from the west.
Twelve shillings a week instead of eight.
Cadernid ffydd.
See the upshot:
rain that runs on the smashed stones
a drinker from a broken cup.

Christopher Meredith

MR FLINT

When I was a boy in Tredegar
I ran errands for the grocer
whose name was Mr Flint.
A shilling on Saturday he gave me
for delivering bacon and eggs.

Flies buzzed all over his shop,
we swatted them with rolled-up comics
and they fell from the air
to land on the sawdust floor.
Butter and cheese were stacked
with sacks of coffee-beans in the corner.
He spoke Welsh, and good English too,
and had never been out of Tredegar.

When my mother was short of cash
he gave her bacon and butter
with bread and cheese and pickles
until she was able to pay.
He helped all the wives of miners
who were out of work at the pit.
Kind Mr Flint, he gave us
bull's eyes and toffee apples.

The shop is gone now
and so is Mr Flint.
All over our country
the shiny new supermarkets stand.
But they do not give food
if you have no money
and they do not give the children sweets.

John Tripp

TORIAD Y WAWR

Pan mae mantell nos yn cuddio
   Ffurf, a lliwiau, daear faith,
Daw y wawr o'i ystafell wisgo,
   Mewn distawrwydd at ei gwaith.
Yn ei gwisg o lwyd oleuni,
   Daw yn gyntaf atom ni,
Ond cyn hir daw'r nef i wenu
   Dan ei seirian wenau hi.

Egyr ddorau'r dydd yn araf,
   I roesawu'r huan têr.
Ffoi o'i wyddfod am y cyntaf,
   Wna byddinoedd mawr o sêr;
O mor brydferth yw ei weled,
   Fel yn dilyn llwybrau'r wawr,
Ac yn edrych mor sirioled,
   Ar breswylwyr daear lawr.

Mae y byd fel pe'n ymysgwyd
   O afaelion cwsg yn awr;
Clywch y ceiliog o'r adarglwyd,
   Yn croesawu toriad gwawr;
O, mor swynol i'r cystuddiol,
   Ydyw gwên y wawrddydd dlos;
Daw a bywyd adnewyddol
   Ac mae'n dranc i dduwch nos.

Gwentwyson

BREAK OF DAY

When the cloak of night hides
  The shape and colours of this mighty earth,
The dawn proceeds from its dressing room,
  Silently going about its work.
In its garment of grey light
  It comes to us at first,
But ere long heaven smiles
  Beneath dawn's glittering smiles.

It slowly opens the portals of day,
  To welcome the bright sun,
The vast armies of stars flee
  Quickly from its presence;
O how beautiful its sight
  Following dawn's paths,
And looking down so cheerfully
  At the inhabitants of the earth.

The world seems to shake off
  Sleep's grasp now;
Hear the cock crowing from its perch
  Welcoming the break of day;
O how charming the sweet smile of dawn
  To the afflicted;
It brings renewed life
  And ends night's gloom.

Translated by the Editor

NOTES ON THE WAY TO THE BLOCK

There's a good crowd here today
to see me off.
I never knew I had so many friends
or enemies. I see several
familiar faces, and breasts.
There's one cariad smiling
whose knickers I took off
long ago in West Tredegar.
I don't see anyone crying.

Well now to get down
off this bloody cart.
A few in the crowd
give me a helping hand,
eager to speed my departure.
Nice of them. I never knew
I had so many friends.

The sun is shining
but the birds have gone.
Birds can sense a bad scene.
The crowd is silent, a bit awed
but looking forward to the experience.
I mount the steps, alone,
see from the corner of my eye
the executioner approach
wearing a jester's cap and bells.
Good. We don't want black
or melancholy at a time like this.

His axe looks sharp.
I give him a cigar to make it clean and quick.
Don't I get a last request
like a joint or a slug of whisky?
Someone in the crowd giggles,
but I can hear one woman weeping.
I take a last look at the sky.

John Tripp

THE STARS OF MEXICO
(An old Chartist remembers)

They call me Jack the Fifer and I come from Nantyglo,
And I played my fife for freedom not so many years ago,
When we took the People's Charter to the gates of
    Newport town,
When we marched to win a Kingdom, and the soldiers
    shot us down.
And sometimes I remember the grey skies of Nantyglo
As I spread my trooper's blanket 'neath the stars of Mexico.

In green and gracious valleys among the hills of Gwent
We never saw the sunshine, to earth our backs were bent,
Like a toiling slave an early grave was all we had to gain,
So we struck like men and struck again, but our struggle
    was in vain.
And sometimes I remember how we dealt that final blow
As I march to other battles 'neath the stars of Mexico.

The month it was November and all the storm winds blew,
And as we marched to Newport, full many of us knew
That our comrades would be lying at the rising of the sun
Who'd never feel its warmth again, nor hear our rivers run.
But we shouldered pike and musket as onward we did go
And we marched as bold as any in the wars of Mexico.

They'd have hanged me as a traitor, so I crossed the stormy
    sea
And I play my fife in a better life in the land of liberty.
For the cruel laws of England I do not give a damn
And I'm shouldering my rifle 'neath the flag of Uncle Sam,
And I'm marching as a soldier in the War of Mexico
To a place I've never heard of, and it's called the Alamo.

They call me Jack the Fifer and I come from Nantyglo.
I always was a fighter and I'll always strike a blow.
With the Stars and Stripes above me, I'll make a soldier's
stand
And not disgrace my ancient race, nor dear Wales, my native
land
And I'll take her honour with me, though fate may lay me
low
Far distant from my homeland, 'neath the Stars of Mexico.

Harri Webb

TÝ'R AGENT, YNYSDDU

The nettle nods where Islwyn used to write,
The rough grass grows where Islwyn saw the Light,
The Light beyond the fading light we know,
The Light Eternal, where no nettles grow.

Idris Davies

AT YNYSDDU

There were two surprises for us
On the road that day. First
The mill, the one I should have known
Because of the name Cwmfelinfach;
And then, as the road arched upward
Over the mass of the hill, the bluebells
Studding the hedges all the way down
Past Islwyn's house. Unexpected
Finding them there, and commoner too
Than willow herb on banks, in ditches,
Beside the sudden stream, the school –
Heads of a vivid, spiky blue
That held us with their beauty, yet
Seemed alien for it somehow,
Out of place. I went expecting
The Big Tip and the shadowed streets,
The crumbling chapels with their high
Inscriptions hammered out in Welsh
All but forgotten. I saw them too.
But, driving to work each day, it was
The bluebells that I noticed, those
That come back every spring, the old
Promise to be true made good
Again and again. Turning my head,
I hoped to raise my eyes. Instead I saw
Only our own the alien now.

Graham Thomas

THE NIGHTINGALE

Methought it all a tale
About the nightingale,
Until she paid one heavenly night
A visit to my vale.

Oh! newer every note,
More thrilling from the throat
Than fairy poesy's drowsy dream
Had ever heard or wrote.

Deep was the briary brake,
Deep was the limpid lake,
But deeper flowed her lay along,
Oh! deeper sunk her song.

I noted all the night
Each lay of rich delight,
Caught every string and every strain,
But never could her tune retain.

Was sorrow e'er so sad
As in her nether note?
Was ever gleeful joy so glad
As when her voice with melody mad
Did on the fleet clouds float?

Islwyn

Y DDERWEN

Ti welaist lawer oes
   Cyn hon, O dderwen eon,
A llawer canrif bell a roes
   I ti ryw heirdd fodrwyon;
 A'u cadw'n ffyddlon byth wnei di
O gariad at yr oesau fu.

A oedd yr oesau fu
   Yn well na'r ganrif hon?
'Rwy'n tybied wrth dy olwg di
   Fod hiraeth yn dy fron
Am fore ddydd canrifoedd gwell,
Canrifoedd dy ieuenctid pell.

A oedd melysach cân
   Yn nofio ar y gwynt
Fu'n chwifio'th ddeilen ieuanc lân
   Ryw ganrif fore gynt?
Oedd! oedd! a minnau gyda thi
Sy'n wylo am y pethau fu.

                      Islwyn

THE OAK TREE

You have seen many an age
   Before, O brave oak tree,
And many a distant century gave
   You some beautiful rings;
You keep them faithfully for ever
Out of love for ages past.

Were those ages past
   Better than this century?
From your looks I think
   There is a longing in your breast
For the morning of a day from more illustrious centuries,
The centuries of your distant youth.

Did some sweeter song
   Float on the wind
That fluttered your graceful young leaf
   In some long distant century?
Ay! Ay! and I too
Weep with you for the things that have been.

Translated by the Editor

Y STORM
(Extract)

Mae'r oll yn gysegredig, mae barddoniaeth
Nefolaidd yn coroni'r bryniau draw.
A bu – goddefer y wladgarol nwyf –
Bu llawer brawd a chyndad hoff i mi
(Nad edwyn neb eu henwau, neb eu clod
Ond taweledig rith yr oes a'u dug)
Ar hyd y bannau hyn ar lawer nawn
Yn canu neu yn wylo fel y caed
Profiadau bywyd. Ninnau gyda hwynt
Adawn gymynrodd o atgofion pêr,
Rhyw anadliadau a myfyrion syn
I'r awel dyner eu mynwesu fyth,
Neu fyth i wylo yn y niwl uwchben.
Pa beth yw Ffynnon Jacob? Y mae delw
Un mwy na Jacob ym mhob ffrwd trwy'r byd.
Fe aeth fy nhadau dros yr afon hon
A'r holl awelon nefol lawer gwaith,
A'r lloer, a llawer seren ddwyfol wawr,
A'r haul, a'r daran hefyd. Mae y byd
I gyd yn gysegredig, a phob ban
Yn dwyn ei gerub a'i dragwyddol gainc.
Ac nid yw glannau yr Aegean bell
Ond rhannau bychain o farddonol fyd.
Ni chanodd Homer am y bryniau draw,
Ni welodd hwynt. Beth fuasai'r Wyddfa hen
Pe cysgodasai hi ei gawell ef?
Rhyw odidocach Ida yn ei gân
A dydd o dduwiau'n torri ar ei brig.

Islwyn

THE STORM

Everything is sacred, yonder hills
Are crowned by a heavenly poetry.
And – may my patriotism be allowed –
Many a brother and forefather dear to me,
Whose names and fame are known to no one now,
Silent phantoms of the age that bore them,
Have sung or wept according to life's experiences
Along these mountains at many a noontide.
We like them will leave a legacy
Of sweet memories, an inspiration and
Astonished thought for the gentle breeze
To cherish ever, or fade
For ever in the mist above.
What of Jacob's well? A greater far
Than Jacob is imaged in every stream
Throughout the world.
My fathers crossed this very river
And all the heavenly breezes many a time,
The moon and many a star of light divine,
The sun and thunder too. All the world
Is sacred, and every mountain bears
Its cherub and eternal song.
And even the remote Aegean shores
Are but small parts of the poetic world.
Homer never sang of yonder hills,
He never saw them. What would old Snowdon be
If she had sheltered his cradle?
A far more splendid Ida in his song
And a dawn of gods breaking on her peak.

                              Translated by the Editor

HAPUS DYRFA

Gwêl uwchlaw cymylau amser,
   O fy enaid, gwêl y tir
Lle mae'r awel fyth yn dyner,
    Lle mae'r wybren fyth yn glir.
     Hapus dyrfa
   Sydd yn nofio yn ei hedd.

Ynddi tardd ffynhonnau bywyd,
   Trwyddi llif afonydd hedd
I ddyfrhau ei broydd hyfryd,
   Ac i anfarwoli ei gwedd;
    Iachawdwriaeth
   Ar ei glan anedlir mwy.

Saethau'r bedd ni allant esgyn
   I'w hagosaf dalaith hi;
Ac ni faidd y marwol elyn
   Sangu ar ei rhandir fry;
    Cartref bywyd,
   Cartref anfarwoldeb yw.

Troir awelon glyn marwolaeth
   Oll yn hedd tu yma i'r fan,
Try holl ocheneidiau hiraeth
   Yn anthemau ar y lan;
    Syrth y deigryn
   Olaf i'r Iorddonen ddu.

Nid oes yno neb yn wylo,
   Yno nid oes neb yn brudd,
Troir yn fêl y wermod yno,
   Yno rhoir y caeth yn rhydd;
    Hapus dyrfa
   Sydd â'u trigfa yno mwy!

JOYOUS MULTITUDE

See above the clouds of time
 O my soul, see the land
Where the breeze is always gentle,
 Where the sky is always clear.
  Joyous multitude
 Floating in its peace!

There the springs of life are welling,
 There flow the rivers of peace,
To refresh its lovely places,
 And to immortalize its beauty;
  Salvation
 Upon its shores is breathed.

Death's arrows are not able to rise
 To its nearest province;
And the mortal enemy dare not
 Tread this region of the skies;
  Life's home
 It is our immortal home.

The breezes of death's vale
 Turn to peace there
All the sighs of longing
 Turn to anthems on the shore;
  The last tear
 Into Jordan's darkness falls.

No one weeps there,
 There no one is sad,
Wormwood there is turned to honey,
 The captive is set free;
  Joyous multitude
 Who will live there ever more!

Mae fy nghalon brudd yn llamu
O orfoledd dan fy mron,
Yn y gobaith am feddiannu
'R etifeddiaeth ddwyfol hon.
Hapus dyrfa
Sydd â'u hwyneb tua'r wlad!

Islwyn

My heavy heart leaps
   Rejoicing in my breast,
In the hope of possessing
   This divine inheritance.
     Joyous multitude
   With their faces towards the land!

Translated by the Editor

HIRAETH AM GRIST

Dymuniad taer pob Cristion yw
Cael eiste'n llon, tra fo fe byw
Dan gysgod Crist, y pren sy'n llawn
O ffrwythau pêr dymunol iawn.

Mae hiraeth llawn, heb amau llai,
Yn llanw pawb o'r duwiol rhai,
Am Grist eu caer a'u cyfaill mwyn,
O tyred Arglwydd, gwrando'n cwyn.

Mae calon pob rhyw Gristion gwan
Yn mawr sychedu am gael rhan
Yng Nghrist a'i gariad, er gwellhad,
O rhyfedd yw fod hwn yn rhad!

Y sawl sy'n profi hyfryd flys
Am Iesu Grist, caent hwy'n ddilys
Baradwys ddisglair, draw i'r bedd,
A gweled wyneb Duw mewn hedd.

Edmund Williams

A LONGING FOR CHRIST

Every Christian's fervent wish is
To sit joyous while he lives
In Christ's shadow, the tree that's full
Of sweet, delicious fruit.

A deep longing uncomplicated by doubt
Fills all the godly,
For Christ their stronghold and gentle friend,
O come Lord, listen to our cry.

Every weak Christian's heart
Thirsts for a part
Of Christ and his love to gain strength,
How strange that this is free!

Those who have a sweet longing
For Jesus Christ will surely find
A bright paradise beyond the grave
And see God's face in peace.

Translated by the Editor

DAU HEN DRIBAN

Mi dreuliais lawer diwrnod
Ar lan Sirhywi wiwglod,
I dynnu cnau ar frigau'r fro,
A thwyllo'r glân frithyllod.

Mi fûm i sbel yn pwdlo
Cyn dechrau gyda'r moldio,
Yn cadw tân i'r injan flast,
A thrin harn cast, a'i lwytho.

Anonymous

TWO TRADITIONAL VERSES

I've idled many a day
On the banks of lovely Sirhowy,
Gathering nuts from the vale's branches,
And tricking the splendid trout.

For a while I was a puddler
Before becoming a moulder,
Tending the fire for the blast furnace,
And treating and loading cast iron.

Translated by the Editor

FROM RISCA WITH LOVE

I'm a citizen of Mummersher,
I'm as English as the Queen,
And I ates them rotten Welshies
Wot paints the signposts green.

I've always lived in Mummersher,
Now they wants to call it Gwent,
But I can't pronounce that ard foreign word,
It do make my teeth all bent.

I ates their orrid language
Wot I can't understand,
It should be a crime to speak it,
I'd like to see it banned!

There's no room for it in Mummersher
Wot's as English as Surrey or Kent,
Though I've eard there's schools wot teaches it
And there's kids wot thinks they're in Gwent.

Just ark at em jabbering at it
Like monkeys in a zoo!
Talk English tidy we gotto, innit,
Like wot ew an me do do.

                                        Harri Webb

CYWYDD I IFOR HAEL

Ifor, aur o faerwriaeth
Deg yw'r fau, diagr o faeth;
Myfi yw, ffraethlyw ffrwythlawn,
Maer dy dda, mawr yw dy ddawn.

Ys dewr, ystyriol ydwyd,
Ystôr ym, ys da ŵr wyd.
Telais yt wawd tafawd hoyw,
Telaist ym fragod duloyw.
Rhoist ym swllt, rhyw ystum serch,
Rhoddaf yt brifenw Rhydderch.
Cyfarf arf, eirf ni'th weheirdd,
Cyfaillt a mab aillt y beirdd.
Cadarn wawr, cedyrn wiwryw
Caeth y glêr, cywaethog lyw.

Dewraf wyd a gwrddaf gŵr
Dy ddilyn, dieiddilwr.
Da oedd a syberw dy ach;
Duw a fedd, dau ufuddach
Wyd i'th fardd, pellgardd pwyllgall,
Llywiwr llu, no'r llaw i'r llall.

Myned o'm gwlad, dyfiad iôr,
Â'th glod, a dyfod, Ifor.
O'm iaith y rhylunieithir,
Air nid gwael, arnad y gwir.
O'm pen fy hun, pen-cun cyrdd,
Y'th genmyl wyth ugeinmyrdd.
Hyd yr ymdaith dyn eithaf,
Hyd y try hwyl hy haul haf,
Hyd yr hëir y gwenith,
A hyd y gwlych hoywdeg wlith,

IFOR THE GENEROUS

Ifor, fair stewardship's gold
Is mine, delightful nurture.
I too, bountiful ruler,
Am your steward, you're much blessed.

It's a grand, you are mindful,
Store for me, you're a fine man.
I paid you the tongue's sweet praise,
You paid me bright dark bragget.
You gave coin, friendly gesture,
I name you "The Generous".
Strong blade, no blades restrain you,
Comrade and bondsman of bards.
Mighty prince, mighty lineage,
Captive of bards, wealthy lord.

You're the bravest, fiecest man
To follow, a strong fellow.
Fine and proud's your pedigree;
God knows, you're twice as docile
To your bard, no dishonour,
Warlord, as this hand to that.

I leave my land, noble branch,
With your praise, I come, Ifor.
From my speech comes the image,
No base word, of what you are.
From my mouth, lord of many,
Multitudes will sing your praise.
As far as man may journey,
As the summer sun can roam,
As far as the wheat is sown,
As far as fair dew moistens,

Hyd y gwŷl golwg digust,
Hydr yw, a hyd y clyw clust,
Hyd y mae iaith Gymraeg,
A hyd y tyf hadau teg,
Hardd Ifor hoywryw ddefod,
Hir dy gledd, hëir dy glod.

Dafydd ap Gwilym

As far as a clear eye sees,
It's keen, far as ear's hearing,
As far as Welsh is spoken,
And as far as fine seeds grow,
Handsome, courteous Ifor,
Long sword, your praise will be sown.

Translated by Joseph Clancy

ENGLYNION I LYS IFOR HAEL

Llys Ifor Hael, gwael yw'r gwedd – yn garnau
    Mewn gwerni mae'n gorwedd,
    Drain ac ysgall mall a'i medd,
    Mieri lle bu mawredd.

Yno nid oes awenydd, – na beirddion,
    Na byrddau llawenydd,
    Nac aur yn ei magwyrydd
    Na mael, na gŵr hael a'i rhydd.

I Ddafydd gelfydd ei gân – oer ofid
    Roi Ifor mewn graean,
    Y llwybrau gynt lle bu'r gân
    Yw lleoedd y dyllhuan.

Er bri arglwyddi byr glod – eu mawredd
    A'u muriau sy'n darfod;
    Lle rhyfedd i falchedd fod
    Yw teiau ar y tywod.

Ieuan Brydydd Hir

TO THE HALL OF IFOR THE GENEROUS

The hall of Ifor the Generous, how mean it looks – mounds
    Lying in a marsh,
  Thorn and blasted thistle possess it,
  Bramble where was once greatness.

No inspiration comes there – no poets,
    No festive tables,
  No gold within its walls,
  No gift, no generous man to offer it.

For Dafydd, skilled in song – a cold sorrow
    To lay Ifor in the earth,
  The paths of long ago once full of song
  Are now the owl's place.

Despite the fame and short-lived glory of lords – their
                                  greatness
    And their walls perish;
  A strange place for pride
  These houses built on sand.

                        Translated by the Editor

MAESALEG

Y carw'n pori megis gynt
    O glawdd i henglawdd hyd y stâd,
Heb ond fy hunan ar ei hynt,
    Na thrydar telyn yn y wlad;
Gwae fi o geisio tloted plwy,
Heb Ifor yn ei Henllys mwy.

Nid fod y drain o'm cylch yn drwch,
    A'r ysgall gwyllt yn lledu 'i wraidd,
Ond gweld Maesaleg falch yn llwch
    Sy'n gwanu 'nghalon drist i'w chraidd;
Nid cwrlid rhôs mieri a drain
Wnai'r tro'n lle deurudd Morfudd gain.

Fe all mai dan y deiliach glas
    Sy dan fy nhraed mae lloriau'r wledd
Lle bu rhianedd uchel dras
    Yn llon ar ddil y tant a'r medd;
Mwy oerllyd fil pan gofiwyf hyn
Yw cri'r dyllhuan yn y glyn.

Mae'r hengoed eto yn y fro
    Yn wern ac yw a deri glas,
Ond ni ddaw Dafydd yno am dro
    I garu a chanu i ferch y Plâs;
Mud, mud, er's talm yw'r Awen bur
Fel bedd y Bardd yn Ystrad Fflur.

Yn iach, Faesaleg lwyd dy wedd,
    I wyndai clyd Morgannwg af,
Ac ar aelwydydd llwm di-wledd,
    Cerdd goll y Llys pwy ŵyr na chaf;
Yn iach; 'rwy'n clywed gyda hyn
Y delyn bêr rhwng muriau gwyn.

                                                    Crwys

BASSALEG

The deer grazing as of yore
   From hedge to old hedge along the estate,
With no-one but myself on their trail,
   Nor the sound of harp anywhere;
Woe is me for seeking such a poor parish,
With Ifor no longer in his old Mansion.

It was not the dense thorn surrounding me
   Nor the wild thistle spreading its roots,
But seeing proud Bassaleg in the dust
   That pierced my sad heart to its core;
The moor's coverlet of bramble and thorn
Was poor compensation for fair Morfudd's two cheeks.

Perhaps under the green leaves
   Beneath my feet are those festive floors
Where high-born maidens
   Made merry with harpstring and mead;
When I remember this a thousand times more chill
Is the owl's cry in the valley.

The old trees remain here –
   Alder and yew and green oak,
But Dafydd no longer comes
   To sing and woo the maid of the Mansion;
Silent, silent, for ages past his perfect Muse
Like the Bard's grave in Strata Florida.

Farewell, grey-featured Bassaleg,
   I'll to Glamorgan's snug white cottages,
And in bare cheerless homes,
   Who knows but I may hear the lost song of the Hall;
Farewell; I hear with this
The sweet harp sounding between white walls.

Translated by the Editor

NEAR BASSALEG

In May the lane was a place of astonishing clarity;
sky, blue as a bruise; foliage
a thrusting green sea parting for me, sole Israelite,
waist-deep in miraculous crossing.
Cow-parsley, like the foam on waves; dog-mercury;
Jack-in-the-Hedge; blue sage;
stitchwort; campion; mugwort – its clenched flowers tight
as fists. And over Pen-y-lan a buzzard's rigid swing.
Now it is a roundel in the stained-glass of memory,
an illuminated miniature on a page
long since turned, colours too bright
to be real, rich smells unconvincing.
And yet it must have led somewhere, the path through the
    sea,
swishing in behind, drowning the distant army.

Catherine Fisher

FROM CLARENCE BRIDGE, NEWPORT

Esk. Isca. Usk. Every day
mud sculpted to fresh form,
river-grain breaking, according
to the tide, tentatively,
violently at the stone feet
of the bridge. This afternoon
gulls cry under the arches, white
as wreaths of effluent,
plastic, feathers which turning tides
lay at the monument. No one
waits here. Wind bandages my mouth.
From melting snows of Ebbw,
Honddu, Usk, Sirhowy
processions of icy air
file to the sea, threading under
and over the bridges crying
a hymn of wind and water.

                                Gillian Clarke

CEFN MABLI

Yma bu pob rhyw lendid mab a merch
    Ar anterth awr eu bywyd yn rhoi tro;
Bu yma ddawns a chân yn cymell serch
    Nosweithiau'r haf i fynwes gwyrda'r fro,
A llygaid mwyn ar lawer trannoeth blin
    Drwy'r ffenestr hon yn gwylio'r curlaw llwyd
A hwyr sigliadau duwch llwm y pîn,
    A thruan dranc cyfaredd yr hen nwyd.
Awgrym nid oes o'r maith rialti gynt
    Nac atgof prin o'r hen anobaith hardd, –
Dim ond rhyw lais yn lleddfu ar fin y gwynt
    A rhosyn gwyllt yn hendre rhos yr ardd,
Ychydig o'r hen wylo yn y glaw,
Ychydig lwch yn Llanfihangel draw.

W.J.Gruffydd

CEFN MABLY

Here the youthful beauty of boy and girl
   In the prime of life had its turn;
Here dance and song aroused the passions
   Of the young men of the vale on summer evenings,
And gentle eyes on many a tired morrow
   Watched through this window the grey pelting rain
And later the shaking of the bare black pines,
   And the sad end to the enchantment of the old passion.
There is no hint now of the past's long riotous hours
   Nor even a precious memory of the old sweet despair, −
Only a voice moderating the sharp wind
   And a wild rose in the garden's winter plot,
A little of the old weeping in the rain,
A little dust in Michaelston church yonder.

Translated by the Editor

THE DIESEL TO YESTERDAY

There is downpour, always,
    as the carriages inch into Newport:
perhaps six times in ten years
    of a hundred visits to custom,
the entry to my country is uncurtained
    by rain or mist. I look
at the shambles of sidings and streets,
    the rust of progress and freight wagons,
the cracked façades of bingo cinemas.
    Sometimes I expect to see
the callous peaked caps and buttons
    of visa-checkers, cold sentries
on a foreign border, keeping out the bacillus
    in hammering rain and swirling fog.
Often I wish it were so, this frontier sealed
    at Chepstow, against frivolous incursion
from the tainting eastern zones.

Patience vanishes with frayed goodwill
    at the sight of the plump bundles
tumbling into Wales.
    They bring only their banknotes
and a petrol-stenched lust for scenery
    to shut in their kodaks,
packing out the albums of Jersey
    and the anthill beaches of the south.
They stand in line for pre-heated grease
    in the slums of crumbled resorts,
nose their long cars into pastureland
    and the hearts of ancient townships
that now are buried under chromium plate.

I catch myself out in error, feel
     ignoble in disdain.
The bad smell at my nostril
     is some odour from myself –
A modern who reeks of the museum,
     not wanting his own closed yesterday
but the day before that,
     the lost day before dignity went,
when all our borders were sealed.

John Tripp

DAYS THAT HAVE BEEN

Can I forget the sweet days that have been,
    When poetry first began to warm my blood;
When from the hills of Gwent I saw the earth
    Burned into two by Severn's silver flood;

When I would go alone at night to see
    The moonlight, like a big white butterfly,
Dreaming on that old castle near Caerleon,
    While at its side the Usk went softly by:

When I would stare at lovely clouds in Heaven,
    Or watch them when reported by deep streams;
When feeling pressed like thunder, but would not
    Break into that grand music of my dreams?

Can I forget the sweet days that have been,
    The villages so green I have been in;
Llantarnam, Magor, Malpas, and Llanwern,
    Liswery, old Caerleon, and Alteryn?

Can I forget the banks of Malpas Brook,
    Or Ebbw's voice in such a wild delight,
As on he dashed with pebbles in his throat,
    Gurgling towards the sea with all his might?

Ah, when I see a leafy village now,
    I sigh and ask it for Llantarnam's green;
I ask each river where is Ebbw's voice –
    In memory of the sweet days that have been.

                                W.H.Davies

THE CHILD AND THE MARINER
(Extract)

In this old captain's house I lived, and things
That house contained were in ships' cabins once;
Sea-shells and charts and pebbles, model ships;
Green weeds, dried fishes stuffed, and coral stalks;
Old wooden trunks with handles of spliced rope,
With copper saucers full of monies strange,
That seemed the savings of dead men, not touched
To keep them warm since their real owners died;
Strings of red beads, methought were dipped in blood,
And swinging lamps, as though the house might move;
An ivory lighthouse built on ivory rocks,
The bones of fishes and three bottled ships.
And many a thing was there which sailors make
In idle hours, when on long voyages,
Of marvellous patience, to no lovely end.
And on those charts I saw the small black dots
That were called islands, and I knew they had
Turtles and palms, and pirates' buried gold.

W.H.Davies

THE COLLIER'S WIFE

The collier's wife had four tall sons
   Brought from the pit's mouth dead,
   And crushed from foot to head;
When others brought her husband home,
Had five dead bodies in her room.

Had five dead bodies in her house –
   All in a row they lay –
   To bury in one day:
Such sorrow in the valley has
Made kindness grow like grass.

Oh, collier, collier, underground,
   In fear of fire and gas,
   What life more danger has?
Who fears more danger in this life?
There is but one – thy wife!

W.H.Davies

THE KINGFISHER

It was the Rainbow gave thee birth,
   And left thee all her lovely hues;
And, as her mother's name was Tears,
   So runs it in my blood to choose
For haunts the lonely pools, and keep
In company with trees that weep.

Go you and, with such glorious hues,
   Live with proud Peacocks in green parks;
On lawns as smooth as shining glass,
   Let every feather show its marks;
Get thee on boughs and clap thy wings
Before the windows of proud kings.

Nay, lovely Bird, thou art not vain;
   Thou hast no proud, ambitious mind;
I also love a quiet place
   That's green, away from all mankind;
A lonely pool, and let a tree
Sigh with her bosom over me.

W.H.Davies

LEISURE

What is this life if, full of care,
We have no time to stand and stare.

No time to stand beneath the boughs
And stare as long as sheep or cows.

No time to see, when woods we pass,
Where squirrels hide their nuts in grass.

No time to see, in broad daylight,
Streams full of stars like skies at night.

No time to turn at Beauty's glance,
And watch her feet, how they can dance.

No time to wait till her mouth can
Enrich that smile her eyes began.

A poor life this if, full of care,
We have no time to stand and stare.

W.H.Davies

BY HENLLYS CHURCH

The bird that on the beechen height above
   No finer thing could do than spend the gold
Of the rich sunset on a song of love
   And so enlarge the wealth a thousand fold
Is silent, since the day's sad, farewell smile
   Ushered the fragrant dusk ... and distant streams
Hold now my ears' attention to beguile
   My mind with music from the realm of dreams.
Remote here seems the world; no sound of strife.
   The swallows are asleep beneath the eaves
Of the old church, where spring the dead to life
   As slowly through the linnet-haunted leaves
The night in solemn beauty now appears
To find her stars reflected in her tears!

Huw Menai

TWM BARLWM

was it here
above the dull drone of motorway
making towns touch
though no hands clasp in fellowship

  was it here
girthed by the planned monotony
of same streets, houses,
parallelograms where people play
at being machines

  was it once, on Twm Barlwm
that long ago this mound
felt the warm pulse of land and sky
sea and stars in its own small cavern

  was it here, where townfolk clamber to the peak
to say they stood above the crowd
on Twm Barlwm
that the last sage keepers of
Celtic mysteries plotted their own
straight ways to the gods with
arcs and angles finely drawn to the heavens,
instruments arcanely tuned to untold harmonies

  then, stones were fired with life
and the curious web of pools and ditches,
trees and mountains strung
over the earth, caught music like an ancient harp

  now, the round hill slumbering
waits for a wanderer to stand
and look and listen –

for there is more to see and hear on
Twm Barlwm than the roads we built
or the bleak symmetry of chapels

Colin Palfrey

THE FOLLY, PONTYPOOL

High where the hill holds heaven in her hands,
High above Monmouthshire the grey tower stands.

He is weather-worn and scarred, and very wise,
For rainbows, clouds and stars shine through his eyes.

He was young for a hundred years, now he is old,
And his bones of stone rattle and crack with cold.

He who was proud and strong now shelters sheep;
He is weather-worn and scarred and full of sleep;

And he stares at space with a grave, octagonal frown,
While winds tear and tug at his crumbling crown.

He who is intimate with the ways of the moon,
And has known sun-ecstasy on a summer noon,

Now gives his dreams to the earth and the sky to keep –
He is weather-worn and scarred and kind to sheep;

And he wraps his head in mist lest he should see
The pathos of his own senility.

Myfanwy Haycock

THE CANAL NEAR PONTYPOOL

Long, liquid miles
That bend and twist and creep
Darkly and imperturbably
Along,
Shallowly silver,
Bewilderingly deep,
Like a slow, green song.

The old canal –
Where sudden noises plop!
And then have never been,
And where
Twisting and twinings
Never seem to stop –
There's magic there;
Dragonfly magic
And gay forget-me-nots,
And strange rat-rustlings
In hidden holes,
While glassy water glints
Suddenly on dark dots
That are tadpoles.

Around the hills,
The little hills and ridges,
Mazed with meandering, it goes.
And swirls
Back on its tracks,
Threading its bridges
Like grey pearls.
Porcelain swans
On weed-green water glide
Inscrutably along,

While slender trees
Talk, talk incessantly
To trees on the other side.

The fat brown bees
Are grumbling
In a warm brown monotone
Among the meadowsweet and mint.
The grass
Leans water-wards,
Flower-tangled and wind-blown,
To see eels pass,
Sinuously.
The captive towpath trudges
Acquiescently between
Water and trees.
A swallow lightly skims
The waterway, and smudges
Reflections of trees.

Long, liquid miles
That bend and twist and creep
Darkly and imperturbably
Along,
Shallowly silver,
Bewilderingly deep,
Like a slow, green song.

                                        Myfanwy Haycock

CARAVANS AT DAWN

Blue and orange caravans, large and bright and lumbering,
Lurched along the lane today while yet the air was cool;
And all the little villages were mazed and warm with
    slumbering,
While caravans went by upon the road to Pontypool.

Autumn mists were in the air and all the grass was glistening,
Trees stretched out their slender arms and shook them free
    from rain,
And someone trilled a merry song when nobody was
    listening,
While all the magic cavalcade went jolting up the lane.

Where the willows wept in sleep the brook had ceased its
    chattering,
Every tiny wind and leaf was very, very still,
When suddenly the air was filled with clashing and with
    clattering,
And blue and orange caravans came trundling down the hill!

Creaking wheels and cracking whips, pots and pans and
    crockery,
Rattled through the hamlet where folk still lay a-bed;
And flaunting gipsy girls leaned out, their eyes aglow with
    mockery,
While old Twyn Barlwm wrapped the clouds more snugly
    round his head.

All the little villages were warm and mazed with slumbering,
Everything was silent and the morning air was cool,
When blue and orange caravans, large and bright and
    lumbering
Made all things seem enchanted on the road to Pontypool.

Myfanwy Haycock

TELL ME

Tell me, is there snow at home,
And do my lovely mountains lie
Like great white fallen angels there
Beneath a numb and sorrowing sky?
And is there winter in the woods
Where nothing, nothing seems to live?
And have you sensed the quietness
That only trees and snow can give?

Have drips and drops of water turned
To long glass fingers overnight?
And, closely pressed against the wall,
Is one frail jasmine star alight?
Do starlings scream upon the roof,
And does the chubby robin wait
Upon the sill, just like a bright
Red apple on a cold white plate?

Do tomtits swing, pale blue and gold,
Upon the bare forsythia branch?
Do clouds with kindly fingers stroke
The furrowed forehead of Pentranch?
And have the hungry sheep come down
From mountain tracks, and do they roam
Like timid ghosts around the town?
Tell me, is there snow at home?

Myfanwy Haycock

Abergavenny and the Black Mountains

THE TOWN WHERE I WAS BORN

The town where I was born is surrounded by hills.
When the evening sky shone turquoise in summer, with
    small ribs of cloud,
And Venus wobbling its brilliance on the horizon,
The hills became solid black without any depth.
Even a farm light gave no perspective, or the lamps of a car
Bumping up to a flash then disappearing
As it twisted down a lane between banks and trees.
And when the night was grey with cloud from the
    Llangattock Mountains
To the Black Mountains across the Usk,
The hills were muggy and insecure, withdrawn without
    feature,
Except over the Blorenge where the under-surface of cloud
had a reddish tinge
From the flaring of blast-furnaces in the town beyond.
There was a steady glow, with occasional flickering, like a
    colour of silence,
And I had to strain to think of the roar and shouts
As liquid steel trundled overhead in cauldrons on chains
To be poured with a shower of sparks in moulds
By men who moved quickly in the heat and glare.
Now things are different: I am another man and look at
    other hills.
Last night I stood on the doorstep after dark and stared into
    the east as if it were the past.

I could guess where Craig-y-Pistyll plunged down
And where was Bryn Garw among the invisible folds,
But all was embedded in dark. I thought: it is without and
    within,
Watching a car on the long track from Banc-y-Darren
Travel down through Cefn Llwyd, faltering lights that rose to
    a glare,
As if they were looking for something.
This time the cloud glowed too, and because the wind had
    veered
through the day from south to east,
I could smell them burning, Birmingham and Coventry,
And the red glowering of the sky was the reflection of their
    flames,
And across Pumlumon, Liverpool and Manchester, and across
    Mynydd Epynt,
Cardiff and Bristol. The cloud slid steadily above me
And on the wind there was the smell of the fine dust of
    bricks
And the black dust of charcoal, and the grey dust of stones.
I never knew before how the smell of cities burning
Is like the must and acridity of old houses and the lives they
    have given up.
I remembered how in Cardiff after the war, we passed rows
    of façades
And nothing else standing, and how in a second-floor
    window for a year
There was a wine-glass intact, missed by the blast,
Placed there by the hand which had drained it and moved
    away
With a shining clarity, a salute and goodbye.

                                        John Barnie

HOME TOWN

I think of the widows; closed flowers.
Who will find them lovely, remembering
Life in the withered petals of their lips?
In morning coffee rooms
They crowd like memories, sunnily.
The make-up and the perms suggest
Summer frocks and jaunts before the war.
Now they tread to church and pray
For company. They are delicate, like moths
Found clinging to the panes on autumn
Nights. Their powdered cheeks are soft
As downy wings. Their eyes glitter
Like gems in faded boxes, blue, green,
And on fire, as many years ago.

John Barnie

SUMMERHOME (ii)

Landscape is revelatory. I know this
independent of poets. – "Cambrensis";
earth-piled, turreted, a border land
of ditch and dyke where Dore Abbey stalks
St. Mary's 'cross fields that blaze like icons.
Sentinel belfry, barely visible 'midst
bulbing greens, the coalescent manifold
haw smothering the hedge's crosshatch; the
sheep chalked on her napkin green; the brown trout
pencilled in his brook. – Orcop, Wormbridge, Much
Marcle. Skirrid Fawr: this "Deheubarth". We
recite names like a litany, plunder our
word-hoard in this scenery which has no landlord
save imagination. And here its archive.

Mark Harrell

BRAD Y FENNI

"Dewch," medd cennad balch de Breos,
    "Dewch, fy ngwyrda, draw i'r wledd,
Bydd y barwn yn eich aros
    Heno heb na helm na chledd.
Y mae'r seigiau oll yn barod –
    Ni bydd sôn am gad na chur;
Chwi gewch yno gwmni hyglod
    Heb na chledd nac arfau dur."

"Diolch," medd Seisyllt, "fo i'r barwn
    Am gwrteisi mwyn a moes;
Down am un-nos ac anghofiwn
    Frwydrau a fu'n chwerwi'n hoes."
Buan gwelwyd Seisyllt eon
    Gyda'i wŷr yn mynd i'r wledd;
"Gwae," medd rhywun yng Nghaerllion,
    "Iddo fynd heb helm na chledd!"

Wrth fynd heibio i'r hen borthcwlis,
    Croeso cynnes a gânt hwy,
Gwae na wyddai'r cwmni hwylus
    Na chaent fyned allan mwy!
"Dewch, bwytewch ac yfwch, wyrda,"
    Mynych y daw'r alwad daer,
Y mae mwy na digon yma –
    Eiddoch chwi yw stôr y gaer!"

THE ABERGAVENNY MURDERS

"Come," said de Breos' proud messenger,
   "Come, my good men, to the feast,
The baron awaits you
   This evening without helmet, without sword.
The delicacies are all prepared –
   There will be no talk of battle or assault;
You will have some famous company there
   Without sword, without steel weapon."

Seisyllt answered, "Many thanks to the baron
   For his gentle and civil courtesy;
We shall come for one night and forget
   The battles that have embittered our lives."
Soon the brave Seisyllt was seen
   On his way to the feast with his men;
"Woe betide him who goes without helmet,
                    without sword,"
   Says someone in Caerleon.

As they pass by the old portcullis,
   They receive a warm welcome,
Alas little did the cheerful band know
   They would never leave thereafter!
"Come, eat and drink, good men,"
   The earnest plea is often heard,
"There is more than enough here –
   The castle's store is yours entirely."

Clywir llais y delyn yno,
  Mwyn a llawen yw pob gŵr,
Melys hefyd ydyw gwrando
  Ar gitâr y trwbadŵr.
"Lleddwch hwy!" – "Ba frad sydd yma?" –
  Dacw'r barwn ar ei draed!
Gwae y Cymry – wedi'r gwledda
  Caiff y cledd ei wledd o waed!

"Lleddwch hwy!" fel taran heriol
  Syrth y geiriau ar eu clyw,
Ac o gwmni'r glewion siriol,
  Un yn unig a gaiff fyw.
Heddwch fo i'th lwch, de Breos,
  Talodd Duw i ti am hyn,
Nid oes dim o'th waith yn aros,
  Ond y castell ar y bryn!

Trefin

The sound of the harp is heard there,
   Every man is gentle and jolly,
It is also sweet to listen
   To the troubadour's guitar.
"Kill them!" – "What treachery is here?" –
   There's the baron on his feet!
Woe betide the Welshmen – after the banquet
   The sword shall have its own feast of blood!

"Kill them!" like thunder
   The murderous words ring out
And from the cheerful band of brave men
   Only one will survive.
Peace be unto your dust, de Breos,
   God has paid you for this,
Nothing of your work remains,
   Only the castle on the hill!

Translated by the Editor

I BLAS SYR RISIART HERBART, COLBRWC

A oes unplas yn siampler?
Oes, un, fal yr haul a'r sêr:
Y tŵr y sydd fal tŷ'r sêl
Ar barc sych o'r brics uchel.
Yr Herbart yn rhoi eurbyrth
A'i gwnâi'n uwch nog Einion Yrth.
Syr Risiart, seiri'r Asia
Ni wnaent ryw dŵr mewn tir da.
Ni wnâi ddyn ei annedd iach,
Ni wnâi lawnter alontach.
Athro gynt a wnaeth ryw gell,
Ei dŷ annedd yn dunnell;
Bwrw rheolaeth bro'r heulwen
Y bu drwy bib wydr â'i ben.
Er meddiant Alecsander
Ni roes hwn awyr a sêr.
Syr Risiart Herbart hirbost,
Athro Gwent, a wnaeth ryw gost,
Cyfryw wydr yn cyfredeg,
Castell fal y dunnell deg.
Gweithio y mae, rhag wythwynt,
Gwaith Fferyll ar gestyll gynt.
Uwch yw'r to na chyriau'r tir,
Uwch yw yntau na chantir.
Uwch na thŵr yw'r milwr mau,
Uwch yw Powls na chapelau.
Deuryw adail dihareb,
Dwy lys hwn a dalai Sieb:
Ehangwen yng Ngefenni
A'i chwaer yn gyfuwch â hi.
Perced i'r ieirll yw'r parc draw,
Plas Arthur, palis wrthaw.
Tŵr gwydr i Ector gadarn,
Tir Gwent bell torrai gant barn.

IN PRAISE OF COLDBROOK,
SIR RICHARD HERBERT'S MANSION

Is there a model mansion?
One stands out, like sun and stars:
Situated in dry parkland,
Its watch-tower built of bricks.
Herbert installed golden gates,
Einion Yrth's were less splendid.
Asia's masons did not raise
Such a well-proportioned tower.
No one could build a grander house
Nor fashion a lovelier lantern.
An ancient philosopher
Chose a tub for his dwelling;
He kept at bay the sun's power,
Sheltered in his glass-made cask.
To the mighty Alexander
He yielded not sun and stars.
The tall Sir Richard Herbert,
Our philosopher of Gwent,
Built an expensive abode
For himself with many windows.
He builds castles to withstand
Strong winds, and so did Virgil.
The roof commands the horizon,
He himself is very tall.
My hero's of towering height,
As is St. Paul's clock-tower.
His two magnificent houses
Would not look amiss in Cheapside;
Ehangwen in Gefenni
And Coldbrook, its worthy twin.
The latter is like Arthur's Court,
A fit home for earls, in parkland.

Mae obry naw tŷ'n y tŵr,
Mae fry ganty ac untwr.
Tref fawr mewn pentwr o fain,
Tŷ beichiog o'r tai bychain.
Ei gaerau yw'r graig eurin,
Ei grib sy goch fal grâbs gwin.
Cerfiwyd a grafiwyd yn grych
Cyrff y derw fal crefft eurych.
Llys goed a main oll ysgwâr,
Llawn gwydr, meillion ac adar.
O'r llys hon mae'r holl synnwyr,
A llew Gwent oll, oll a'i gŵyr.
I'r tŵr a wnaeth, nis tyrr neb,
Y doeth annedd doethineb.
Pwy a wnâi synnwyr pen well
Eithr y dyn aeth i'r dunnell?
Pwy un gorff â'm penaig i?
Pwy yw patrwn pob poetri?
Piau'r holl gampau pei rhaid,
Pob rhinwedd? Pab barwniaid.
Gwent alarch a gân telyn,
Ac a rydd aur am gerdd ynn.
Ni bydd ef, myn bedd Ifan.
Heb rôt a liwt, Herbart lân.
Awn at organ y Teirgwent,
I Ynys Wydrin, gwin Gwent.
Elment im, fal maen Tomas,
Y dyw'r plwm a'r gwydr a'r plas,
Yn grwybr yn y gaer obry,
Yn gorfau cyfrwyau fry.
Nid oes wyneb, dwys anun
Yn y lamp na welo'i lun.
Gweled drych y mae'n gwlad draw,
Gŵyl Gwent ei golwg yntaw.

The mighty Hector in this fortress
Of Gwent could repulse a throng.
There are nine rooms on ground level,
Many other rooms above.
This great house is a noble pile,
Providing shelter for many.
Its ramparts are golden-hued,
Its roof's like red grapes in colour.
Its oak beams have rough carvings
And craftsmen have gilded them.
'Tis a court of wood, stone and glass.
Surrounded by birds and clover.
This court is the fount of all skills,
All pay tribute to Gwent's lion.
There will be no breaking in
To this abode of wisdom.
Who makes better sense of things
Than today's Diogenes?
Who equals my chief in stature?
Who is the patron of bards?
Who excels in all the feats
And virtues? The pope of barons.
The swan of Gwent plays the harp,
And pays us gold for our paeans.
I swear that the noble Herbert
Will never lack rote and lute.
The three cantrefs are ruled from here,
From Gwent's Isle of Avalon.
I feel as if I'm at home
In this honeycombed mansion.
Its lead, its glass, its columns
Give a philosopher's stone's light.
All sorts of folk, good and evil,
Can gain self-knowledge in its glow.
It is a mirror, spied from afar,
In it Gwent sees its reflection.

Bid wydr i'r byd i'w edrych,
A brawd i'r Iarll biau'r drych.

Guto'r Glyn

Let the whole world look into it,
The Earl's brother owns the mirror.

Translated by Dyfnallt Morgan

LLYS LLANOFER

I hwn bu hen arglwyddi'r wlad
    Yn cyrchu o bob tu,
I gael mwynhad o'r delyn fâd –
    Hen delyn Cymru Fu.

Ac i lys hael Llanofer gynt
    Y cyrchai llawer bardd,
A chroeso gwir i feirdd y tir
    Oedd yn ei neuadd hardd.

Yn hwn y cadwyd llyfrau heirdd,
    'Sgrifennwyd er cyn co' –
Trysorau'r iaith, am gyfnod maith,
    Fu 'nghadw tan ei do.

Ac yno bu Gwenynen Gwent,
    Ar ddydd Gŵyl Ddewi Sant,
Wrth fwrdd y wledd yn llon ei gwedd,
    Yn gwrando ar gân y tant.

O! dedwydd oedd y dyddiau gynt
    Pan oedd uchelwyr gwlad
Yn parchu'r iaith, ddydd gwyl a gwaith,
    A charu'r delyn fâd!

I gael yr heniaith eto'n ôl,
    Llafuriwn nos a dydd,
O, boed y tant tan ddwylo'r plant
    I foli Cymru Fydd!

                                 Trefin

LLANOFER HALL

The country's lords came
   To this hall from all corners,
To take pleasure in its splendid harp –
   The old harp of Wales's past.

And to generous Llanofer Hall
   Came many poets of the land,
Who were made most welcome
   In its handsome hall.

Fine books were kept here,
   Books written long ago –
For many years the treasures of the language
   Were housed here.

And here Gwenynen Gwent
   Would on Saint David's Day
Sit feasting at table
   Enjoying the sound of the harpstring.

Oh happy days long ago
   When the nobles of the land
Respected the language on feast and workday,
   And loved the splendid harp!

We shall labour night and day
   And hear the old language once again,
May the children pluck the harpstrings
   In praise of the future Wales.

Translated by the Editor

CAN MLYNEDD I NAWR

O deffro fy awen o ddyffryn cysgodrwydd,
    Lle buost yn llechu, rho weled dy wawr;
Y tafod sy'n 'awr yn dy annerch mor hylwydd,
    A drig mewn distawrwydd, can mlynedd i nawr.

Can mlynedd i nawr, 'roedd rhai o fy nheidiau –
    Yn wridgoch ei gruddiau, eur lwythau ar lawr;
Ond heddiw yn gorffwys yn dawel mewn beddau,
    'R un modd byddaf finnau can mlynedd i nawr.

Rhyw fyd cymysgedig yw'r byd ag wyf ynddo –
    Weithiau yn llawen ac weithiau yn drist;
Weithiau mewn gwisgoedd sidanaidd yn rhodio,
    Ac weithiau'n newynog heb geiniog 'n y gyst.

Weithiau rhwng tonnau a chreigiau echryslon,
    Bryd arall rhwng meillion, rhai gwyrddion eu gwawr;
Fel hyn 'rwyf yn teithio, rhaid cofio, i'r ceufedd, –
    Lle byddaf yn gorwedd can mlynedd i nawr.

Pe rhoddid holl berlau yr India ddwyreiniol,
    A chyfoeth gwlad Affric- Americ- i mi;
A chael breniniaethu ar bawb o'r hil ddynol,
    Ar orsedd eirianol wiw freiniol o fri;

A rhodio'r dinasoedd mewn cerbyd o arian,
    A phawb i ymostwng i mi hyd y llawr; –
"Gwagedd o wagedd" – a fyddent, y cyfan.
    Gadawent fi'n unig can mlynedd i nawr.

A HUNDRED YEARS FROM NOW

Awake my muse from shadow's vale,
  Where thou hast been lurking, reveal thy dawn,
The tongue that now greets thee so eloquently,
  Will be silent a hundred years from now.

A hundred years from now, some of my forefathers –
  Were rosy cheeked, earth's golden generation;
But today they rest silently in their graves,
  As I shall a hundred years from now.

The world I am in is a confusing one –
  Sometimes merry and sometimes sad;
Sometimes wandering dressed in silken clothes,
  And sometimes hungry and penniless.

Sometimes amid waves and dangerous rocks,
  At other times in clover, green of hue;
Like this, let it be remembered, I journey to the grave –
  Where I shall rest a hundred years from now.

If I were given all the pearls of the East Indies,
  And the wealth of Africa – America;
If I were to rule over the whole human race,
  On a fine, bright throne of privilege and fame;

And if I were to journey through cities in a silver coach,
  With everyone bowing low to me;
All would be vanity, all vanity,
  I should be lonely a hundred years from now.

Dos di, y credadun, ar dy bererindod, –
　Er cwrdd a bwystfilod a llewod y llawr; –
Ymwroled dy galon, cryfhaed dy ysbryd –
　Cei fil gwell cyfeillion can mlynedd i nawr.

Can mlynedd i nawr dy ffydd droir yn olwg –
　A'th obaith, sy'n wanllyd, yn hyfryd fwynhad;
Can mlynedd i nawr cei weled yn amlwg,
　Yr hyn mewn addewid a roddodd y Tad.

Cei sefyll yn wrol ar fryniau Caersalem, –
　Cei goron i'th ben, a thelyn i'th law;
Rhy faith fyddai enwi'r dedwyddwch anrhaethol
　A fydd yn dy feddiant can mlynedd i nawr.

Eiddil Gwent

Thou, the believer, go on thy pilgrimage –
    Though thou encounter beast and lion,
Embolden thy heart, strengthen thy spirit –
    Thou shalt have much better companions a hundred
                                   years from now.

A hundred years from now thy faith will grant thee sight –
    And thy weak hope will become a sweet pleasure;
A hundred years from now thou shalt clearly see,
    What the father's promised gift will be.

Thou shalt stand bravely on Jerusalem's hills –
    A crown on thy head, a harp in thy hand;
Impossible to name the ineffable bliss
    That will be thine a hundred years from now.

                       Translated by the Editor

BEDD Y DYN TYLAWD

Is yr ywen ddu ganghennog
   Twmpath gwyrddlas gwyd ei ben,
Fel i dderbyn o goronog
   Addurniadau gwlith y nen;
Llawer troed yn anystyriol
   Yn ei fathru'n fynych gawd,
Gan ysigo'i laswellt siriol:
   Dyma fedd y Dyn Tylawd.

Swyddwyr cyflog Gweithdy'r Undeb
   A'i hebryngodd ef i'w fedd,
Wrth droi'r briddell ar ei wyneb
   Nid oes deigryn ar un wedd.
'N ôl hir frwydro â thrafferthion,
   Daeth i ben ei ingol rawd:
Noddfa dawel rhag anghenion
   Ydyw'r bedd i'r Dyn Tylawd.

Mae'r garreg arw a'r ddwy lythyren
   Dorrodd rhyw anghelfydd law
Gydchwaraeai ag e'n fachgen,
   Wedi hollti'n ddwy gerllaw;
A phan ddelo Sul y Blodau,
   Nid oes yno gâr na brawd
Yn rhoi gwyrdd-ddail na phwysïau
   Ar lwm fedd y Dyn Tylawd.

Ar sedd fynor nid yw'r Awen
   Yn galaru uwch ei lwch,
A chyn hir drwy'r las dywarchen
   Aradr amser dynn ei swch;
Un â'r llawr fydd ei orffwysfa,
   Angof drosti dynn ei rhawd;
Ond er hynny, angel wylia
   Ddaear bedd y Dyn Tylawd!

Ioan Emlyn

THE PAUPER'S GRAVE

Beneath the dark spreading yew tree
  A grassy-green mound lifts its head,
Ready to receive the royal
  Adornment of heaven's dewfall;
Countless heedless feet
  Have often trampled messily on it,
Crushing its beautiful verdure:
  Ah! 'tis but the Pauper's grave.

Hirelings from the Workhouse
  Bore him to his grave,
When they shovelled earth over him
  Not a tear was shed.
After long battles against tribulation
  His life's joyless course came to an end:
A peaceful refuge from want
  Is the Pauper's grave.

The rough headstone with its two-lettered epitaph
  Carved by some unskilful hand,
Belonging to a playmate of his youth,
  Lies split in two on the ground;
And when Palm Sunday comes,
  No loved one, no brother,
Comes to lay green leaf or flower
  On the Pauper's lonely grave.

No Muse on marble seat
  Mourns above his dust,
And soon through the green turf
  Time's plough will urge his share;
One with earth will be his resting place
  Oblivion will soon take its course;
Yet for all this, an angel shall keep watch
  Over the Pauper's grave.

                      Translated by the Editor

BORDER COUNTRY
(Extract)

Whichever route we take, we lose the way:
After the trout-farm, for instance, when the lane
Keeps leading us along the valley floor
Until it hops the stream to climb a while,
Only to descend and re-negotiate
The maze of meadows in the stream's vicinity.
Winding on through alders, then avoiding
Pine and larch plantations, it continues
Dithering until it reaches Llanthony.
Here I doubt the road: it ought to climb,
Since I remember some amazing views;
And so reverse, to turn and then retrace
The single track till Cwmyoy reappears,
Its tower askew by landslip or design,
Suggesting how a head should hang aslant
When hands are nailed – and yoy is Welsh for yoke.
Above the weathered hamlet which it serves,
The sliding mountain has a yoke-like look:
And where a yoke would dip to fit a neck
Monks on mules brought bitter through the gap
From Longtown which is just across the border.
However, this is not the time to stop:
When I reach the cross-roads, I go left,
Then left again, to crawl behind some ponies
Carrying a trekking party upwards:
Little girls with curls which do not fit
Their velvet-covered riding caps, with glasses
Bouncing on the bridges of their noses.
At the top of this steep stretch of hill
The tarmac peters out: we're forced to stop,
While the Black Mountains claim the riders.
Now we've got no option but to roll
Down the lane and take the route abandoned.

Right, then right again, and back we go
Upon the tracks we just retraced, along
The by-road which meanders with the stream,
Slowing at its bends and backing up
For motorcades descending from the pass
Presumably some distance up ahead of us.
Flitting by a stand of twisted sycamores
We swerve to miss a pheasant, notice bulls
And buzzards, come again to Llanthony,
And pass the point beyond the Half Moon pub
At which I lost my nerve, with Offa's Dyke
Above us on the ridge which marks the border
Separating undulating Hereford
From the bald, escarping hills of Gwent.
Later, though, the blackest hill of all
Bulges at us through a perfect blaze
Of hawthorn blossom slashed at by the wipers.
Rising well above two thousand feet,
This knob is dubbed Lord Hereford's – the Tumpa.
It's a steep, uncompromising bump
Giving the impression of a camel:
Like it, lump it, there's no easy way
To scale the thing, and Dilys says at once,
Derek's mountain! Derek is a painter
Haunted by this gloomy shape: it stumps him
And looms up, an image in his mind
Often seen through such a blaze of hawthorn.
On we go, though, since our guiding stream
Winds around it; then we start to climb
On and up and ultimately over
Gospel Pass, to meet the panorama
Taking in both Hereford and Powis
Laid out like one's crumpled bed at breakfast.

Ploughed fields, whale-backed hills, dingles
Moving into ever more be-misted
Visionary vales beyond the Wye
Looping round the bookshop town of Hay.
High above the larches, we are partly
Made of sky, we feel, as we look down:
As if we'd left the ground and joined the blue,
Or balanced on some line between the two.
And later, coming back from Hay, with loot
Sufficient for a bookstall in the boot,
We thunder briefly, as we cross the grid,
Ascending steeply, and encounter mist
Before we reach the ridge, its sluggish density
Has left a chilling trail, a slime of frost
On every mound of turf along its path.
Flakes of snow drift singly to the screen
And disappear. The whiteness keeps us mute.

Anthony Howell

FIESOLAN MUSINGS
(Extract)

Where alders mourn'd their fruitless beds
A thousand cedars raise their heads,
And from Segovia's hills remote,
My sheep enrich my neighbour's cote.
The wide and easy road I lead
Where never paced the harnest steed,
Where hardly dared the goat look down
Beneath her parent mountain's frown,
Suspended while the torrent-spray
Springs o'er the crags that roll away.
Cares if I had, I turn'd those cares
Toward my partridges and hares,
At every dog and gun I heard
Ill-auguring for some truant bird,
Or whisker'd friend of jet-tipt ear,
Until the frighten'd eld limpt near.
These knew me, and 'twas quite enough,
I paid no Morning Post to puff,
Saw others fame and wealth increase,
Ate my own mutton-chop in peace,
Open'd my window, snatcht my glass,
And, from the rills that chirp and pass,
A pure libation pour'd to thee,
Unsoil'd uncitied Liberty!
Lanthony! an ungenial clime,
And the broad wing of restless Time,
Have rudely swept thy massy walls
And rockt thy abbots in their palls.
I loved thee by thy streams of yore,
By distant streams I love thee more;
For never is the heart so true
As bidding what we love adieu.

Yet neither where we first drew breath,
Nor where our fathers sleep in death,
Nor where the mystic ring was given,
The link from earth that reaches heaven,
Nor London, Paris, Florence, Rome,
In his own heart's the wise man's home,
Stored with each keener, kinder, sense,
Too firm, too lofty, for offence,
Unlittered by the tools of state,
And greater than the great world's great.
If mine no glorious work may be,
Grant, Heaven! and 'tis enough for me,
(While many squally sails flit past,
And many break the ambitious mast)
From all that they pursue, exempt,
The stormless bay of deep contempt!

Walter Savage Landor

A DAVID JONES MURAL AT LLANTHONY
(for Jeremy Hooker)

Rain had turned the countryside
into a sump. From Capel-y-ffin
that constant, dripping screen obscured the hills,
drowning a file of ramblers
and swallowing two sad pony-treks.
I sheltered under sopping oaks,
then lifted a latch into a long
monks' larder, with boxes of bad apples, oranges,
mouldy biscuits and cake,
a mysterious pyramid of fresh eggs.
On the stone lay a splintered carafe
crusting a sediment of wine at the base.

Then I saw it . . .

Delighted, I remember thinking:
if the dealers receive wind of this
they'll climb here with mallets and chisels.
It was a signed
original, flaking fast on a cracked wall –
the dark buff and faded red of his fine
leaning script, the numerals of Rome,
a Christian head and a believer's praise embedded in the
    text.
Time and neglect were chipping at beauty, scraping a
    masterpiece.

(He had walked this corridor,
studied the portraits of Tudor martyrs,
put his brushes on the floor beside me,
and gazed at the Black Mountains.
A few days, fifty years before,

occupied his mind and hand
to leave us a lost symbol
like some flourish of hope.
Feeling, wondering, testing, watching,
seeing clues in fragments –
"For it is easy to miss Him
     at the turn of a civilisation".)

Six winters from the Flanders mud
he came here, looking for a slot
of peace, some method to preserve sanity.
Deep reticence after misadventure
informed his plan; the chronicles that unlocked his horror
were yet to be written.
All that complexity,
the full bulging yield of myth
was growing as he painted on a monastery wall –
history to be sacked, language to be made,
the honours far off, and the life
continuing, aimed at the past.

Its price brought the long
loneliness, to be lived through in a Harrow room,
for one soldier of goodness and truth.

John Tripp

THE RIVER USK AND THE PASTORAL HEART OF GWENT

THE BANKS OF YSCA

'Tis day, my crystal Usk: now the sad night
Resigns her place as tenant to the light.
See the amazed mists begin to fly
And the victorious sun hath got the sky.
How shall I recompense thy streams, that keep
Me and my soul awaked when others sleep?
I watch my stars, I move on with the skies
And weary all the planets with mine eyes.
Shall I seek thy forgotten birth and see
What days are spent since thy nativity.
Didst serve with ancient Kishon? Canst thou tell
So many years as holy Hiddekel?
Thou art not paid in this: I'll levy more
Such harmless contributions from thy store
And dress my soul by thee as thou dost pass,
As I would do my body by my glass.
What a clear, running crystal here I find:
Sure I will strive to gain as clear a mind,
And have my spirits – freed from dross – made light,
That no base puddle may allay their flight.
How I admire thy humble banks: nought's here
But the same simple vesture all the year.
I'll learn simplicity of thee and when
I walk the streets I will not storm at men,
Nor look as if I had a mind to cry:
It is my valiant cloth of gold and I.
Let me not live, but I'm amazed to see
What a clear type thou art of piety.

Why should thy floods enrich those shores, that sin
Against thy liberty and keep thee in?
Thy waters nurse that rude land which enslaves
And captivates thy free and spacious waves.
Most blessed tutors, I will learn of those
To shew my charity unto my foes,
And strive to do some good unto the poor,
As thy streams do unto the barren shore.
   All this from thee, my Ysca? Yes, and more;
I am for many virtues on thy score.
Trust me thy waters yet: why – wilt not so?
Let me but drink again and I will go.
I see thy course anticipates my plea:
I'll haste to God, as thou dost to the sea;
And when my eyes in waters drown their beams,
The pious imitations of thy streams,
May ever holy, happy, hearty tear
Help me to run to Heaven, as thou dost there.

Thomas Vaughan

THE WORTHINES OF WALES
(Extract)

A pretie Towne, calde Oske neere Raggland stands,
A River there, doth beare the selfesame name:
His Christall streames, that runnes along the Sands,
Shewes that it is, a River of great fame.
Fresh water sweete, this goodly River yeelds,
And when it swels, it spreads ore all the Feelds:
Great store of Fish, is caught within this flood,
That doth indeede, both towne and Countrey good.

A thing to note, when Sammon failes in Wye,
(And season there goes out as order is)
Than still of course, in Oske doth Sammons lye,
And of good Fish, in Oske you shall not mis.
And this seemes straunge, as doth through Wales appeere,
In some one place, are Sammons all the yeere:
So fresh, so sweete, so red, so crimp withall,
As man might say, loe, Sammon here at call.

A Castle there, in Oske doth yet remaine,
A Seate where Kings, and Princes have bene borne:
It stands full ore, a goodly pleasant Plaine,
The walles whereof, and towers are all to torne,
(With wethers blast, and tyme that weares all out)
And yet it hath, a fayre prospect about:
Trim Meades and walkes, along the Rivers side,
With Bridge well built,the force of flood to bide.

Upon the side, of wooddie hill full fayre,
This Castle stands, full sore decayde and broke:
Yet builded once, in fresh and wholesome ayre,
Full neere great Woods, and many a mightie Oke.
But sith it weares, and walles so wastes away,

In praise thereof, I mynd not much to say:
Each thing decayd, goes quickly out of minde,
A rotten house, doth but fewe favours finde.

Three Castles fayre, are in a goodly ground,
Grosmont is one, on Hill it builded was:
Skenfreth the next, in Valley is it found,
The Soyle about, for pleasure there doth passe.
Whit Castle is, the third of worthie fame,
The Countrey there, doth beare Whit Castles name,
A stately Seate, a loftie princely place,
Whose beautie gives, the simple Soyles some grace.

Two myles from that, upon a mightie Hill,
Langibby stands, a Castle once of state:
Where well you may, the Countrey view at will,
And where there is, some buildings newe of late.
A wholesome place, a passing plat of ground,
As good an ayre, as there abouts is found:
It seemes to sight, the Seate was plact so well,
In elders daies, some Duke therein did dwell.

Carleon now, step in with stately style,
No feeble phrase, may serve to set thee forth:
The famous Towne, was spoke of many a myle,
Thou hast bene great, though now but little worth.
Thy noble bounds, hath reacht beyond them all,
In thee hath bene, King Arthurs golden Hall:
In thee the wise, and worthies did repose,
And through thy Towne, the water ebs and flowes.

Thomas Churchyard

HILL FORT, CAERLEON

From this tree-finned hill
Breasting the breeze –
Leaf shadows like water shifting,
Sounds of water always moving
In the preening of so many leaves –
I can look down over old Caerllion.

In the aqueous rush of bracken fronds
Breaking round, and in a sound
Clearer now, once heard,
An unbroken hum
Like some instrument endlessly strummed
On one low note, or the tone

Of wires looped from pole
To pole vibrating through wood
Where we pressed our ears,
There is a sense of something living,
Breathing, watching here
As I push towards the rampart mound.

The path is blocked. A swarthy
Sentry bars my way, his spear –
Tip sparks with sunlight.
He challenges me in accents I know well;
The words I recognise but the sense eludes.
I am ashamed and silent. He runs me through.

Sam Adams

POEM FOR DAVID LEWIS
(d. 27 August, 1679)

. . . I believe you are met here to hear a fellow-countryman
   speak . . .

You spoke Welsh on the scaffold;
the Usk men understood you.
They would not now.
The local executioner locked his door;
it was a stranger who tightened your
tourniquet of rope,

and then they held him back till you were dead;
would not let the worst be done.
They created saints in their own image;
small men, cunning and discreet,
saints of the kitchen and the gentry's table,
compassionate, unassuming.

David Lewis, priest, Welshman,
wearer of disguises,
look at your grey town and swollen river,
the churches and the muddy lanes,
the houses whose dark hiding-holes you knew.
Look at your people, David,

the women and the young men who still kneel
and kiss the cold unchiselled granite
that marks your March, your borderland,
the bruising ground of language against language,
where the rough rope necklace dropped,
and strangled speech.

                                             Catherine Fisher

SUMMERHOME (iii)

Now watch the sky throw down its pail of milk,
blue milk, poured over a century-long
afternoon. Roaring summer, sun-frazzled,
tesselated, breeding objects that are
brilliant-edged, burning the heart a lobster
red. The day flames into focus: stunned
meadows, a scorched civilization of corn
zig-zag; fields a Byzantine chequer-
board, barleyed gold. High summer, sun-tasseled,
rind-yellow, open. It fires under the
chancel arch of the head. These fields
are our Forum: each parish church
a Saint Peter's: and the Usk, our
Tiber, it sweats to molten lead.

Mark Harrell

MAESTR A MAESTRES WILIAM POWEL
(Extract)

Pwy sy o Went pasa'i wŷr?
Pwy wrtho falpai Arthyr?
Y Maestr Powel a welir
O Lansoe haela'n y sir.
Maestr Wiliam yn meistroli
Mwyn ŵr brau mewn aur a bri.
Hydd o Ddafydd oedd ddifalch,
Ni ffaela byth Phylip walch.
Brytwn dad i dad ydoedd,
Yn iaith Brytaniaid in' oedd.

Gwawr lân o Forgan fawrgost,
A'i bryd ar roi brwd a rhost.
O wraig weddaidd wreigeiddwych!
Un sad, Maestres Fflywrens wych.
Ag ŵyr dau farchog yw, gall;
Ag orŵyr marchog arall;
A chwaer marchog rhywiog, rhwydd,
Eurglod mwy nog un arglwydd.

Dafydd Benwyn

SIR WILLIAM AND LADY POWELL

Who else from Gwent surpasses his name?
Who, compared to him, is like Arthur?
Mr Powell of Llansoy
Is clearly the most liberal in the county –
Mr William commands,
Sweet generous gentleman, in gold and honour.
A humble hart from David he was,
Philip the hawk will never be extinct.
A Briton from father to father he was,
In the language of the Britons to us . . .

A fair lady from wealthy Morgan,
Intent upon giving boiled and roast meat.
Oh! becoming, elegant and wifely wife!
A discreet one, Mistress Florence fine.
And wise, she is the grandchild of two knights;
And the great-grandchild of another knight,
And the sister of a genial, generous knight,
Of golden fame, more than any other lord.

Translated by the Editor

AWDL FOLIANT TRAHAEARN
(Extract)

D'aur ym, Trahaearn fyth a drig – i'm byw,
    mab Ieuan ap Meurig;
  dy glared yn unwedig,
  dy orais fry dros ei frig.

O frig cyff bonheddig hen
    yr oeddych, ac o'i wreiddyn;
  o gerllaw tref Gaerllion,
  o deml Wysg, o Adam lin.

Adam, gwn baham, oedd dy hŷn – fal iarll,
    Rhirid Flaidd o Benllyn;
  o Went y doi'n gynta' dyn,
  ac o Wynedd eginyn.

O Wynedd mae ywch ennill,
    o ddwy Went arfau'n un ddull;
  tri phen saeth a aeth ywch oll,
  tri phen blaidd unwraidd oedd well . . .

    yn eryr i'th lys digrynŵraidd,
    yn dywysog cerdd paradwysaidd;
Ym Mhenrhos Fwrdios, pwy faidd – heblaw hon
  ym mron Caerllion fal carw llewaidd.

                      Lewys Glyn Cothi

ODE IN PRAISE OF TRAHAEARN

Your gold ever continues to my living, Trahaearn,
    son of Ieuan ap Meurig;
  your claret especially,
  your orange aloft above its top branch.

Of a top branch of a noble old stock
    you were, and from its root;
  from near the town of Caerleon,
  from Usk's temple, from Adam's line.

Adam, I know why your ancestor was like the earl,
    Rhirid Flaidd of Penllyn;
  from Gwent he came a foremost man,
  and from Gwynedd an offshoot.

From Gwynedd you have advantage,
    from the two Gwents blazons of the same device;
  three arrow heads that rose above all,
  three wolves' heads of the same root – even better . . .

  an eagle in your stately court,
  a prince of heavenly song,
At Penrhos Fwrdios, who dares besides this one
  on the breast of Caerleon like a lion-hearted stag?

                Translated by the Editor

DERBYSHIRE BORN,
MONMOUTH IS MY HOME

Derbyshire born, Monmouth is my home,
Monmouth I call Wales, for the voices there
Speak in the songs of Welshmen, and the names
Used every day there – Llantarnum, Pontypool,
Tyn Barlwyn, Ebbw Vale –
Are letters from Wales wherever I see them in print.
Caerleon, my youthful home, was a green hill,
A Buddha's belly smiling in a flat field,
Its rondure assimilating for a future age
The marvels of Rome – villas, baths, a bracelet;
And the bridge, too, grey over the yellow Usk,
A thick wide river reminding me of Tiber
In later memory, Tiber unseen,
For Caerleon is all romance and Rome to me –
Brachets and palfreys, the tourney, the hart in the woods,
Imperial roads, the caves of Mithra, fortresses,
And the salt of the ships at Newport and Barry.

Derbyshire born, Monmouth is my home,
Monmouth I call Wales despite cartographers,
My home for a few young years and now,
In spite of Leicestershire that schooled and fought me
And fights me still insisting in my blood.
Yes, Leicester got into my blood and made my bone –
Leicestershire loved me, its stubborn son
Who hated the no man's land, the elbower-out
Of northern and southern culture, possessing none,
I declared in my youthful arrogance:
I saw the cinder paths of mining villages –
Ibstock, Moira, Ellistown –
The chip shop and the corner shop that sold
Racing tips and shameful novelettes;

I saw the dirty pub that loved the colliery
Like its fat and dirtier purse;
And I saw the migrations of miners moving
Across the coalfields from shift to shift
In the red Midland buses they called Red Emmas,
Men's faces black, with rubber-dinghy lips
And floating eyes like nightmare Christy minstrels –
And as I saw I shuddered and cycled on,
Homeless and sick in the towns my home;
Cycled to Charnwood for its hobo roads,
Pre-Cambrian rocks and lonely lapwings,
Rock rose and oak and prairies of fern –
Cycled in solitude to meet a monk
Who stared from a long way off and did not speak.
Charnwood to me was a shape of fear:
Square Teutons of granite, blue jowls
Of bullying slate: I shuddered and ran
To the railway wagons with their owners' names
Painted along their sides like Yankee athletes',
And I was homeless again in Leicestershire.

But Leicester is in my eyes and mind: the Trappist
Tall in the mist, the crags like fangs,
The ruined abbeys, the smell of coal
Have mined in me like secret workings. Monmouth
I choose, but Leicestershire has chosen,
And lucky I am, reluctant, having a home
Today when the world is homeless.

Clifford Dyment

FROSTY MORNING, CAERLEON

Frost has licked the fields clean overnight;
purity, distilled like manna. White lace
cobwebs rattle over the stable doors, abandoned;
coins are rings of ice in my gloves.
This morning the village huddles inwards over its fires,
its toast, its breakfast television,
cold-shouldering – save where the bakery steams
a brief sirocco to pause in and gaze
at the glazed yellow pasties, the hot crusts.
Barracks are cold cubes, unprinted today; the
amphitheatre a white horseshoe
stamped by imperial design.
At the farm cohorts of sparrows cavort in tumbling barns;
cows weave optimistic coats of breath;
dogs chase string; ice is in the milk.
Turning,
I watch the children pour from buses to the school,
roaring over the icy Roman fields;
Barbarians, desperate for warmth.

                                        Catherine Fisher

ROMAN ROAD

This is the way the Romans came,
Steadily, steadily over the hill:
This is the way the Romans came
(And if you listen, you'll hear them still!)
Men from Italy, Africa, Gaul,
Resolute soldiers, strong and tall,
Rome the mother of one and all
Sent them to work her will.

Cohorts, cohorts, with breasts of flame,
(Straight as an arrow-flight over the hill!)
This is the way the Romans came
To build and govern, to sow and till:
Men from Asia, Germany, Spain,
Marching along in sun and rain,
(Forests to fell and fens to drain
And Britons to tame and drill!)

Euphrates, Danube and Nile and Rhine,
(The eagles have drunk their fill.)
Thames and Severn and Forth and Tyne,
(Caerleon just over the hill!)
And this is the way the Romans went,
Their glory fading, their vigour spent,
Over the rolling downs of Gwent,
(Steadily over the hill!)

The road they fashioned pays homage yet
To a splendour that long lies still:
And we that follow must not forget
The Roman courage, the Roman will:
And dreamers hear when the shadows fall
The stirring sounds of their bugle-call,
(Men of the Empire, Romans all,
Marching over the hill!)

A.G.Prys-Jones

TO VALERIA

(A young Roman lady buried at Caerleon during the
Roman occupation of Britain)

How came you to this misty, northern isle
Your Empire's frontier, set amid the foam
Of turbulent winter seas, so far from home,
Where under kindlier skies the sun-god's smile
Ripened your beauty to its radiant hour?
What bonds of love and duty had the power
To draw you from your land of warm delight
In youthful ardour, and with eyes more bright
Than almond-blossom blown on springtide air:
What other cords had failed to keep you there?

Sometimes I see you drooping, see you age
And languish like some brilliant-plumaged bird
Stolen from tropic glades, which says no word
But stares and starves bewildered in a cage:
Valeria, did you sigh and weep and pine
For Tiber and the purple-clustered vine,
The oleander's hues and the rich blue
Of southern seas that summer skies fall through?
Concealing grief beneath your Roman pride,
Could it be thus, Valeria, that you died?

I like to think that long before you went
Into the silence which knows no recall,
You found new happiness which held you thrall
Along these hills and vales of golden Gwent:
And while you walked beside the winding Usk
You saw the fairy folk who dance at dusk,
And heard old melodies upon the air
Plucked from their harps by wandering minstrels there,

And braver music from a prophet's hands
Whose voice declaimed his dreams of wondrous things,
Of people countless as the Tiber's sands
Arising from these shadowy forest-lands,
With great sea-captains, conquerors and kings,
And poets with their winged imaginings,
And teeming cities, miracles to come
When Rome, your mighty mother would be dumb.

Perhaps the changeful beauty of this land
Enchanted you, and as its welcomed guest
You came to love, and then to understand
The brooding mystery of the ancient west:
And songs more poignant than the songs of Italy
Took seisin of your heart and held it true,
So that if ever it were offered you
To live beside the blue Tyrrhenian sea
That moves in silken murmurs tidelessly,
You would have chosen this dear isle again,
This isle, these mountains and the healing rain.

A.G.Prys-Jones

CYWYDD I WILIAM HERBART

Os blaener yn llanner a'n llu,
Os Cymro megis Cymry,
Britwn wyt Herbart o'n iaith,
Bwrw d'olwg lle bu'r dalaith.
Arglwydd o wisg a'i gledd wyd,
Er aros y'th oreurwyd.
Wiliam wayw-wialen wen
Oedd gannwyll ddydd y gynnen.
Dy wên a gâr bob dyn gwan,
Dy win rhugl o'th dai'n Rhaglan.
Rhyfeddod fod rhyw fyddin
Nas gyr Gwent drwy Wysg mo'r gwin.
Addaw a wnaeth ddwyn ieithydd,
Achul gardd a chilio i'r gwŷdd.
Os mawr ysbyty Ieuan,
Mwy dy rent, o mynnud ran.
Prif afon, pery fwyfwy
Hyd y môr, heb gael oed mwy;
Fwyfwy ffyniawdwr ydwyt,
Hyd dy frig llyn dwfwr wyt.
Achubist yn wych hoywbor
O dir mwy nad â i'r môr.
Nid wyd wan, ond dydanydd,
Nid hoffi ei wlad na Thref Ludd.
Alexander mal eryr
Aeth yn wych gynt; ewch a'ch gwŷr.
A chowaeth y'th ddechreuwyd,
Uchlaw dug uchelwaed wyd.
Dring hefyd drwy anghyfiaith
Ffon yn uwch er ffynnu'n iaith.
Gochel gwnsel a gwensaeth
A gwin Sais, gwenwyn sy waeth.
Gwrthefyr gynt, gwarth fu'r gwaith,

TO WILLIAM HERBERT

If there is a leader for us and for our force,
If there is a Welshman who is as Wales itself,
You, Herbert, are the Brython of our nation:
Cast your eye over what has been our realm.
You are majestic in your raiment and your armour,
Gilded for your durability.
William of the gleaming white lance,
The candle in the day of conflict,
Every powerless soul loves your smile
And the flowing wine of your palaces at Raglan:
It is a wonder that no army has been launched
Over the Usk on such a vintage.
He promised to take a compatriot,
A garden sapling removed to woodland.
If great be the estate of John's Hospice,
Yours would be greater, were you to claim your right.
Our main river, flowing wider and wider
To the sea without pause;
Greater and greater, you are a creator of prosperity,
To your brim a lake of wealth;
You have preserved brilliantly a fertile pasture
That nevermore will be swallowed by the sea.
You are strength itself, the comforter,
Having no regard for London nor its country:
As Alexander like an eagle
Arose in splendour, so lead your men.
You have been created by pure workmanship,
You are of superior blood, above dukes;
Climb through all enmity,
Another rung higher for our nation.
Avoid the Saxon's counsel, his white arrow,
And his wine worse than poison.
Remember Vortemir, the vile deed done to him,

Llywelyn felly eilwaith.
Dwg nef yn dy gynefin,
Rho i'th waed dy aur a'th win.
Cadw i'th lys lle y caed wyth wledd,
Gyw'r wennol, gŵr o Wynedd.
Dy ferch yn briod a fo,
A thrwydded a'th aur iddo.
N'ad i do newidio'r dyn,
N'ad i arall dy ederyn.
A fo yn ôl Cadwgon
Yw'r eryr mawr o dir Môn.

Dafydd Llwyd

And again the deed done to Llywelyn.
Live a heaven in your homeland,
Give to your own kin your gold and wine.
Keep in your court of numberless banquets
The swallow's fledgling, the man from Gwynedd;
Grant the hand of your daughter,
Grant your word and your gold to him;
Let not the man be changed by a change of home,
Let no other have charge of your bird;
He, the successor of Cadwgan,
Is the great eagle from the land of Anglesey.

Translated by John Gwilym Jones

PANORAMAS AND CLOSE-UPS
(Castell Rhaglan, Gwent)

Over the swelling waves of rural Gwent
it stands, impassive. Grey sandstone rooted
in living earth. A hard-clenched, distant fist
That none shall pass.

But closer: cross the humbled drawbridge
besieged by busy, Nikon'd tourists, capturing Tuesday
Pass through sky-roofed passages and pigeon-painted walls;
find the hollow hexagon of pitched-stone court

Inside this geometric ruin, history's vulgar joke;
a privy, above an obsidian moat
and glinting dimples of sliding carp

But don't look down, look up
To daylight, and above your head
the Grreat Tower, swaying to the nomad clouds;
filigree arch of ruined window
tufted with random green

Between the looming mass and you
Just where a man might sit (though not in comfort!)
minus newspaper square or entertaining manuscript,
there is a keystone, curved to follow the line of might.
Into the stone, incised, a mark still clear
despite the filter of five hundred years.

A plain and simple crossed-loop fish,
a mason's mark
A prideful, silent shout through time
That common man had skilful hand
in all of this.

Jenny Sullivan

STRAWBERRY PICKING
(Williams' Farm, Raglan)

One field, dew soaked
Bejewelled by early sun
Loud with insistent bees
small creatures
And dawn-crack birdsong.

One field, knitted into rows
of breeze-stirred green
starred with white
And under dark leaves
the heavy, hidden berries

Don't bend: with all this wealth
your back will fail before the fruit

Kneel in the straw-strewn earth
part the leaves – the rash
will come, but later –
and snap the tendril.

Pick the gravid fruit
Place it, sun-warmed, in your mouth
Eyes closed. Then bite.
Release the sweet, sharp, perfumed blood
The sensation
is summer.

Jenny Sullivan

Monmouth and the Wye Valley

THE HUSHING OF THE WYE

The Danube to the Severn gave
  The darkened heart that beat no more;
  They laid him by the pleasant shore,
And in the hearing of the wave.

There twice a day the Severn fills;
  The salt sea-water passes by,
  And hushes half the babbling Wye,
And makes a silence in the hills.

The Wye is hushed nor moved along,
  And hushed my deepest grief of all
  When filled with tears that cannot fall,
I brim with sorrow drowning song.

The tide flows down, the wave again
  Is vocal in its wooded walls;
  My deeper anguish also falls,
And I can speak a little then.

Alfred, Lord Tennyson

MUDDING

When there's danger of flooding,
it's time for the mudding
of doors with low fences
in slots as defences
against tide, windy weather,
and rain all together.

The Wyesider watches
the highest-tide notches,
then brings mud in a bucket,
and when he has stuck it,
he blocks drains and spaces
at low window bases.

He consults his tide table,
Old Moore, and old Abel,
who remembers the flooding
in spite of the mudding,
when the banks were all lower,
and more than one rower
made frivolous sallies
by back streets and alleys,
just to tell future ages
in newspaper pages
as a record or annal,
how the whole Bristol Channel
seemed to rise and deliver
to the bursting grey river
half an ocean of water
sufficient to slaughter
the rats in the cellars
of riverside-dwellers.

When there's danger of flooding,
it's time for the mudding...

Ivor Waters

THE BANKS OF WYE (Extract)

The air resign'd its hazy blue,
Just as Landoga came in view;
Delightful village! one by one,
Its climbing dwellings caught the sun.
So bright the scene, the air so clear,
Young Love and Joy seem'd station'd here;
And each with floating banners cried,
"Stop friends, you'll meet the slimy tide."

Rude fragments, torn, disjointed, wild,
High on the Glo'ster shore are pil'd;
No ruin'd fane, the boast of years,
Unstain'd by time the group appears;
With foaming wrath, and hideous swell,
Brought headlong down a woodland dell,
When a dark thunder-storm had spread
Its terrors round the guilty head;
When rocks, earth-bound, themselves gave way,
When crash'd the prostrate timbers lay.
O, it had been a noble sight,
Crouching beyond the torrent's might,
To mark th' uprooted victims bow,
The grinding masses dash below,
And hear the long deep peal the while
Burst over Tintern's roofless pile!
Then, as the sun regain'd his power,
When the last breeze from hawthorn bower,
Or Druid oak, had shook away
The rain-drops 'midst the gleaming day,
Perhaps the sigh of hope return'd
And love in some chaste bosom burn'd
And softly trill'd the stream along,
Some rustic maiden's village song.

Robert Bloomfield

LINES WRITTEN A FEW MILES
ABOVE TINTERN ABBEY

Five years have passed; five summers, with the length
Of five long winters! and again I hear
These waters, rolling from their mountain-springs
With a sweet inland murmur. – Once again
Do I behold these steep and lofty cliffs,
Which on a wild secluded scene impress
Thoughts of more deep seclusion; and connect
The landscape with the quiet of the sky.
The day is come when I again repose
Here, under this dark sycamore, and view
These plots of cottage-ground, these orchard-tufts,
Which, at this season, with their unripe fruits,
Among the woods and copses lose themselves,
Nor, with their green and simple hue, disturb
The wild green landscape. Once again I see
These hedge-rows, hardly hedge-rows, little lines
Of sportive wood run wild; these pastoral farms
Green to the very door; and wreathes of smoke
Sent up, in silence, from among the trees,
And the low copses – coming from the trees
With some uncertain notice, as might seem,
Of vagrant dwellers in the houseless woods,
Or of some hermit's cave, where by his fire
The hermit sits alone.

                  Though absent long,
These forms of beauty have not been to me,
As is a landscape to a blind man's eye:
But oft, in lonely rooms, and mid the din
Of towns and cities, I have owed to them,
In hours of weariness, sensations sweet,
Felt in the blood, and felt along the heart,

And passing even into my purer mind
With tranquil restoration:- feelings too
Of unremembered pleasure; such, perhaps,
As may have had no trivial influence
On that best portion of a good man's life;
His little, nameless, unremembered acts
Of kindness and of love. Nor less, I trust,
To them I may have owed another gift,
Of aspect more sublime; that blessed mood,
In which the burthen of the mystery,
In which the heavy and the weary weight
Of all this unintelligible world
Is lighten'd:- that serene and blessed mood,
In which the affections gently lead us on,
Until, the breath of this corporeal frame,
And even the motion of our human blood
Almost suspended, we are laid asleep
In body, and become a living soul:
While with an eye made quiet by the power
Of harmony, and the deep power of joy,
We see into the life of things.

                                        If this
Be but a vain belief, yet, oh! how oft,
In darkness, and amid the many shapes
Of joyless day-light; when the fretful stir
Unprofitable, and the fever of the world,
Have hung upon the beatings of my heart,
How oft, in spirit, have I turned to thee
O sylvan Wye! Thou wanderer through the wood
How often has my spirit turned to thee!
And now, with gleams of half-extinguish'd thought,
With many recognitions dim and faint,
And somewhat of a sad perplexity,
The picture of the mind revives again:

While here I stand, not only with the sense
Of present pleasure, but with pleasing thoughts
That in this moment there is life and food
For future years. And so I dare to hope
Though changed, no doubt, from what I was, when first
I came among these hills; when like a roe
I bounded o'er the mountains, by the sides
Of the deep rivers, and the lonely streams,
Wherever nature led; more like a man
Flying from something that he dreads, than one
Who sought the thing he loved. For nature then
(The coarser pleasures of my boyish days,
 And their glad animal movements all gone by,)
To me was all in all. – I cannot paint
What then I was. The sounding cataract
Haunted me like a passion: the tall rock,
The mountain, and the deep and gloomy wood,
Their colours and their forms, were then to me
An appetite: a feeling and a love,
That had no need of a remoter charm,
By thought supplied, or any interest
Unborrowed from the eye. – That time is past,
And all its aching joys are now no more,
And all its dizzy raptures. Not for this
Faint I, nor mourn nor murmur: other gifts
Have followed, for such loss, I would believe,
Abundant recompence. For I have learned
To look on nature, not as in the hour
Of thoughtless youth, but hearing oftentimes
The still, sad music of humanity,
Not harsh, nor grating, though of ample power
To chasten and subdue. And I have felt
A presence that disturbs me with the joy
Of elevated thoughts; a sense sublime
Of something far more deeply interfused,

Whose dwelling is the light of setting suns,
And the round ocean, and the living air,
And the blue sky, and in the mind of man,
A motion and a spirit, that impels
All thinking things, all objects of all thought,
And rolls through all things. Therefore am I still
A lover of the meadows and the woods,
And mountains; and of all that we behold
From this green earth; of all the mighty world
Of eye and ear, both what they half-create,
And what perceive; well pleased to recognize
In nature and the language of the sense,
The anchor of my purest thoughts, the nurse,
The guide, the guardian of my heart, and soul
Of all my moral being.

                  Nor, perchance,
If I were not thus taught, should I the more
Suffer my genial spirits to decay:
For thou art with me, here, upon the banks
Of this fair river; thou, my dearest Friend,
My dear, dear Friend, and in thy voice I catch
The language of my former heart, and read
My former pleasures in the shooting lights
Of thy wild eyes. Oh! yet a little while
May I behold in thee what I was once,
My dear, dear Sister! And this prayer I make,
Knowing that Nature never did betray
The heart that loved her; 'tis her privilege,
Through all the years of this our life, to lead
From joy to joy: for she can so inform
The mind that is within us, so impress
With quietness and beauty, and so feed
With lofty thoughts, that neither evil tongues,
Rash judgments, nor the sneers of selfish men,

Nor greetings where no kindness is, nor all
The dreary intercourse of daily life,
Shall e'er prevail against us, or disturb
Our chearful faith that all which we behold,
Is full of blessings. Therefore let the moon
Shine on thee in thy solitary walk;
And let the misty mountain winds be free
To blow against thee: and in after years,
When these wild ecstasies shall be matured
Into a sober pleasure, when thy mind
Shall be a mansion for all lovely forms,
Thy memory be as a dwelling-place
For all sweet sounds and harmonies; Oh! then,
If solitude, or fear, or pain, or grief,
Should be thy portion, with what healing thoughts
Of tender joy wilt thou remember me,
And these my exhortations! Nor, perchance,
If I should be, where I no more can hear
Thy voice, nor catch from thy wild eyes these gleams
Of past existence, wilt thou then forget
That on the banks of this delightful stream
We stood together; and that I, so long
A worshipper of Nature, hither came,
Unwearied in that service: rather say
With warmer love, oh! with far deeper zeal
Of holier love. Nor wilt thou then forget,
That after many wanderings, many years
Of absence, these steep woods and lofty cliffs,
And this green pastoral landscape, were to me
More dear, both for themselves, and for thy sake.

William Wordsworth

ABATY TINTERN

Pa sawl bron a oerodd yma,
   Pa sawl llygad gadd ei gloi,
Pa sawl un sydd yn y gladdfa
   A'r cof ohonynt wedi ffoi?
Pa sawl gwaith, ar wawr a gosber,
   Swniai'r gloch ar hyd y glyn?
Pa sawl ave, cred, a phader
   Ddywedwyd rhwng y muriau hyn?

Ar y garreg sydd gyferbyn
   A faluriwyd gan yr hin,
Tybiaf weld, o flaen ei eilun,
   Ryw bererin ar ei lin;
Tybiaf fod y mwg o'r thuser
   Eto'n codi'n golofn wen,
A bod swn yr organ seinber
   Eto yn datseinio'r nen.

Ond Distawrwydd wnaeth ei phabell
   Lle cartrefai'r anthem gynt,
Nid oes yma, o gôr i gangell,
   Un erddigan ond y gwynt.
Fel y darffo pob coelgrefydd,
   Crymed byd gerbron y Gwir,
Hedd a chariad ar eu cynnydd
   Fo'n teyrnasu tros y tir.

Alun

TINTERN ABBEY

How many have felt death's chill here,
　　How many eyelids have been closed,
How many lie buried here
　　All memory of whom has fled forever?
How many times at dawn or vespers,
　　Has the bell sounded along the valley?
How many aves, creeds and prayers
　　Have been uttered between these walls?

On the stone opposite
　　Shattered by the elements,
I imagine a pilgrim
　　At prayer kneeling before his image;
I fancy that the smoke from the censer
　　Rises anew in a white column,
And the sound of the melodious organ
　　Resounds afresh in the heavens.

But Silence has encamped
　　Where formerly the anthem was heard,
There is no sound here, from choir to chancel,
　　Except the harmony of the wind.
As each superstition fades
　　The world stoops before the Truth,
Peace and love shall increase
　　To rule over the land.

Translated by the Editor

CHEPSTOW

In the grey Wye waters
the silver tremor of salmon
and track of an otter.

From the moot hall ceiling
still stare the stone faces
of men whose oak ships
sailed for oil and salt
and Gascony wine,
or who bargained for stockfish
on the banned coasts of Iceland,
when Harry of Monmouth
led his bowmen to Agincourt.

Half hidden in oakwoods,
the portwalls and castle
built by the Normans
to hold Gwent in awe.
Here ruled the Bigods,
the Marshals, and Clares,
Lords of the Marches,
unruly to kings.

Stones of nine hundred years,
streets shaped at the Conquest,
narrow disorder
winding up from the river.

Ivor Waters

CHEPSTOW: THE CASTLE
(Extract)

With admiration view yon castle there!
Hung by some necromancer in the air:
High o'er the rocks – see how it lifts its head!
To guard the river Vaga in her bed,
Who far beneath in perfect safety lies,
While her tall giant never shuts his eyes.
Above the castle gate, for ever green,
A vast wide-spreading ivy bush is seen,
Where the grave owl in solemn silence sleeps,
And safe from boys and girls her station keeps.
But quits at night her venerable house,
To find for supper a fat Chepstow mouse;
When found, in haste she stoops upon her prey,
Then back on wabbling wings her murky way
Explores, to shun the dazzling glare of day.
Thus poachers, pest of sportsmen, nightly prowl,
Taught, in the dark, to murder by the owl...
Here cag'd for life, that famous regicide
Well known in Berkshire, Harry Marten died.
Cromwell and he successfully rebell'd,
The father vanquish'd, and the son expell'd:
This very castle Cromwell forc'd to yield,
And chac'd the royal armies from the field.
Charles, when restor'd, gave Marten leave to live,
But freedom to a rebel would not give.
The stern republican disdain'd a grace
That rarely shone in Charles's royal race;
And much displeas'd, that freedom was deny'd,
He spurn'd the worthless boon, and sudden died;
His freeborn soul, in haste, from bondage fled,
T'enjoy unbounded freedom with the dead,
Who in the cause of Britain nobly bled.

On this country never had cried – "Fie on!"
Had he not kill'd, but chain'd, the rampant lion.
Such then is Chepstow Castle – such the case,
Of this once famous – now, old ruin'd place;
Owlets and bats now garrison the fort,
Alone patrol the solitary court:
Dead silence reigns! – here howls no noisy daemon,
To frighten good old Baucis and Philemon;
All here is peace – no matrimonial jar
Disturbs the fort, where roar'd the god of war.

Edward Davies

CHEPSTOW: THE BRIDGE
(Extract)

Near, upon wooden piles, erect and strait,
A bridge is built, that bends beneath our weight.
The startled traveller gives God his thanks,
When pass'd in safety o'er the rattling planks.
This tott'ring bridge fills animals with fear,
Hard is the task to drive them over here.
The sturdy ox, obedient to the goad,
Here quarrels with his driver and the road,
Unwilling moves on this elastic path,
That bends and springs beneath him like a lath.
Here oft the head-strong pig will start aside,
Bounce through the rails and plunge into the tide.
Thus a live fish, when frying, full of ire,
Springs in the pan and leaps into the fire.
Even dogs, by nature bold, are seiz'd with dread
When first on this unstable bridge they tread;
Like cats they crouching creep, turn back, proceed,
Retreat again, then run with all their speed,
And to their masters whimpering declare,
That love for them has triumph'd over fear.
The warlike horse here finds his courage fail,
Keeps at an awful distance from the rail;
Sees through the broken planks the tide below,
Snorts and moves on majestically slow:
Steps in the middle, as the safest way,
Nor feels a wish to caper or be gay:
The drunken clown alone, when passing here,
Sings, and reels on, insensible of fear.

Edward Davies

ST. TEWDRIC'S WELL

Toad on the soft black tarmac knows it's there;
screened by deadnettle, tumbled with ivy.
He enters the water like a devotee,
anointed with bubbles.

If you lean over, your shadow shrouds him;
dimly your eyes find watersnails
down on the deep green masonry, and coins,
discarded haloes.

Tewdric's miracle, not even beautiful,
slowly effacing itself in exuberant nettles,
its only movement the slow clouds,
the sun's glinting ascension.

Lost in the swish of grasses, the hot road,
blown ladybirds, soft notes from a piano;
and over the houses the estuary grey as a mirror,
its islands stepping-stones for Bran or Arthur.

Catherine Fisher

well at TRELLECH

this pool is full of wishes
and salmon under rushes
pass a sunken church
                touching each wall

this pool is full of pebbles
and gently rising bubbles
is it bottomless?
                no echoes call

this child is full of wonder
dropping dreams in water
making faint bells chime
                he hears them all

this child has spent an hour
trying to reach the tower
once more. how far can
                innocence fall?

                            alison bielski

The Severn

invaders

1
this west-bound train gathers speed
blackness clatters at land's gradient
   we descend into Hell
Severn's bed thirty feet under tide
suddenly jerking upwards
        climb into Wales
        so Julius Frontinus I pass that place
where your first footstep shocked Gwent
   Black Rock whose white Shoots
        rush on ebb-tide towards Atlantic

        you scanned green Levels
   sandstone cliffs bleeding crimson
   above grey-bouldered foreshore
Wentwood's twin peaks purple and gold
   challenged you from the north

2
now I walk through centuries
   of pillage and destruction
   to this nuclear power site
I crush buried skulls of servants
   murdered in Harold's intruding palace
   stand on altars cracked by Black Pagans
I pass the arrogant Roman camp
   press new patterns on covering mud
   my briefcase bursts with plans
        to expand Severnside

behind me shadow probes
canisters dumped in this Channel
     mutated fish rise
    bloated battle corpses
tossed on Severn's unharnessed Bore

    this is a shore Julius
that cannot obliterate invasions
    you did not step back
but conquered this land for greed
Black Rock you are the ragged marker
and warning reef of new mistakes
  with these planners I cannot
tread upon your jagged stones
warn them warn Europe before that
    final footstep brings disaster

alison bielski

A DECEMBER NOON

It is as if the day were done, –
   As though the night had come too soon, –
For inky clouds shut out the sun,
   And make a twilight hour of noon.

Through murky moors the misty Usk
   Curves on its immemorial way;
The Holms loom dimly through the dusk –
   Grey islands in a sea of grey.

No flash of gold, no gleam of blue,
   But only pallor, tears, and dearth,
As if some envious spectre threw
   A shroud upon the sleeping earth.

But a breeze springs up; a change begins;
   The sullen cloud bank breaks and drifts;
And, as the shattered greyness thins,
   Quick shafts of radiance pierce the rifts.

And lo! to cheer us, far away,
   A symbol of benignity,
Beyond the blackness and the grey,
   A line of gold upon the sea!

W.J.T.Collins

SEVERN ESTUARY ABC

A is a hat. Sun on my head.
B binoculars I'm using
C across the water. Largest concentration.
D is design. Planned.
E in Europe. Believe that.
F is mud flats, wading birds
G for godwit, green sandpiper, grey plover
H is heavy population, heavy water.
I'm informed. I watch tv. My hat is
Just there to stop the sun burning.
Know what does it?
L is little suns in bottles. Heat.
M is the mighty atom.
N for no trouble in Oldbury, Hinkley Point, Berkley.
Old stuff, I know. They're not sure.
P soup of a public explanation.
Quantity before quality. The fuel of the future.
R is rich someone's salting somewhere. There's always
someone
Severn seeped solid. Sold down the river.
T is truth. Piece of fiction.
Ah yes.
U is understanding. It's safe.
V is very safe. Formation of ducks. Skinhead. Thatcher.
We buy it.
X marks the spot. The insidious ingress. The cancer.
Why don't we do something?
Z is the sound of us listening.

Peter Finch

SEVERN BORE

Somewhere out there the sea has shrugged its shoulders.
Grey-green masses slip, rise, gather
to a ripple and a wave, purposeful, arrowing up
arteries of the land. Brown and sinuous, supple
as an otter, nosing upstream under the arching
bridge; past Chepstow, Lydney; Berkeley where a king
screamed; Westbury, where old men
click stopwatches with grins of satisfaction;
slopping into the wellingtons of watchers,
swamping the nests of coots, splashing binoculars.
And so to Minsterworth meadows where Ivor Gurney's
ghost
walks in sunlight, unforgotten; past lost
lanes, cow-trodden banks, nudging the reeds,
lifting the lank waterweed,
flooding pills, backwaters, bobbing the floats
of fishermen, the undersides of leaves and boats,
and gliding, gliding over Cotswold's flawed
reflection, the sun swelling, the blue sky scored
with ripples, fish and dragonfly, stirred
by the drip and cloop of oars; and finally, unheard,
washing into the backstreets of the town to lie
at the foot of the high
cathedral; prostrate, breathless,
pilgrim from a far place;
refugee
from the ominous petulance of the sea.

Catherine Fisher

THOUGHTS ON HAPPINESS
(Extract)

Severn and Vaga, each old Cambria's pride,
Take different channels down Pumlumon's side.
Destined they seem a separate course to keep
Through rough uneasy windings to the deep.
For if by chance one turns across the plain
In haste to meet its fellow stream again,
Some envious hill or rude projecting rock
Repels its ardour; the repulsive shock
Turns it aside, and with impetuous force
Sends the stream foaming down a different course.
But when no longer obstacles delay
And each impediment is moved away,
Nature in all her varied charms is seen
To hail the union of her river-queen.
Through riven rocks her sportive eddies foam,
Where blue-eyed Naiads keep their hallowed home;
Through blooming orchards winds her mazy flood,
Through deep low vales whose sides are crowned with
wood.
Past Tintern's arches and its mouldering walls
In eager haste her rapid current falls;
Nor does she stay, so great her haste would seem,
To show their image in her rippling stream.
Severn advances in majestic pride
To meet his lost, his long deserted bride.
Vaga well pleased his summons to attend
At Striguil's towers meets her former friend;
Mixed with his wave she seeks his oozy reign
And flows with him to their last home, the main.

Francis Homfray

MISCELLANEOUS

AFTER MY OWN HEART

He skims a flat stone on the sea
and "He's a man
after your own heart." you say.
But I can tell
it isn't thrown for pleasure
but display.

He's crew-cut, bronzed, teutonic-fit,
and sixty plus;
she – in the tracksuit – thirty-five or so.
No wonder that
he wants her to perceive the boy-at-heart
in that sharp, dextrous throw.

It's true my slowing heart still likes
to play the boy.
But if (please don't) you left me free
- died or decamped –
I wouldn't try to make it young again
for such as she.

She – if she came – could gladly have
my knowing heart.
But my stone-throwing heart, my heart that leaps
and runs, remembering
its innocence
is yours for keeps.

Mick Morden

JOINT POSSESSION

When we had stripped the room,
skin after skin down to the wall's clean bone,
we found "Elizabeth" carved there.
The message came,
like light arriving from a distant star,
across a hundred years.

No other house shines near –
the darkness lets you see the distant stars.
There was no other noise
when, in the night,
three times, as we two lay alone, we heard
another climb the stairs.

Once, and again, he rose
and found the stairwell dark and starless space,
no body there. The third time I
went and found words:
"This house is ours now, that we share with you,
and care." The footsteps ceased.

Another tends to floor and stove
with me, sets bread to rise, pegs clothes,
sits in the evening sun
content. We co-exist,
sharing this space though separate in time
like earth and distant star.

Mick Morden

YR EHEDYDD

O'r nyth,
   A'i asgell deg yn llawn o wlith,
   Dyrchafu i fyny megis rhith
     O blith y brwyn
     Mae'r hedydd mwyn,
   I byncio ei foreuol lith.

O'r swyn!
   Sy'n llifo o dy garol fwyn,
     Aderyn bach!
     Dy fiwsig iach,
   A ysgafnha fy loes a'm cwyn.

Os mud
   Yw dan draed yr hunawl fyd,
   Fe'th glywir di yn canu'n glyd
     Ar risiau'r gwawl
     Ddihalog fawl,
   Yn ffrydio o dy heddwch drud.

Mor gu
   A hoenus yw dy osgo di
   Ynghanol ffrwd o heulog li;
     O'r wybren dêr
     Dy gathl bêr
   A seinia fel y mêl i mi.

Ossian Gwent

THE SKYLARK

From its nest
   With its fair wing heavy with dew,
   Ascends phantom-like
      From amongst the rushes
      The sweet skylark,
   To sing its morning song.

Such enchantment
   Flows from your sweet carol,
      Little bird!
      Your wholesome music
   Eases my pain and plaint.

When silence
   Oppresses this selfish world,
   One hears you singing aloft
      On the rays of light,
      A pure song of praise,
   Streaming from your precious peace.

So pleasing
   And lively is your form
   Mid a stream of sunny sea;
      From the bright sky
      Your sweet melody
   Is a honeyed sound to me.

                        Translated by the Editor

IN MONMOUTHSHIRE
(To W.J.T.C.)

Fair country that knew Norman lords and knights,
Sloping towards the Severn lovingly,
What ghosts of devout Friars and Anchorites
Haunt its old ruins when the moon is high!
The sea, that bears the weight of many ships
On trade, adventure, or on pleasure bound,
Seems very calm from here, though from its lips
There comes a low, monotonous moaning sound.
I see bright garments round green bushes furled
Where gypsies camp near peg and basket-wood,
And ply the oldest craft in all the world!
The sky is cloudless, in a happy mood,
The upturned soil is busy in the sun
Swelling to yield the goodly harvest planned –
To yield a hundred grains for every one
Touched by the magic of the tiller's hand.
A river sings! And where the may flies pass
The hungry trout leap in their pools, so clear.
Warm waves of fragrance from the blue-bell mass
Come with the air I breathe; and I can hear
The simple notes of cuckoo and of dove,
Like simple words which tell of simple things –
Sun, moon and star, earth, life and death and love –
That have immortal, elemental wings...
The windy abstract terms of schools no more
Have feudal overlordship! Nature here
Speaks no affected, ornate metaphor
But Bible language that is crystal clear.
A rabbit, its wee tail a magic wand,
Dives for its hole, and I can see again
From her entrancing, nonsense Wonderland,
Alice emerge to find a world less sane.

Blueflies and honeyflies and bumble bees
Conduct their aery orchestras – sweet sound!
The Unseen Soul is full of symphonies –
The all-sustaining Soul which wraps us round –
For humble listeners, alas! too few
In these our noisome demagogic times
Which cannot read the signs of falling dew
Or hear reproachful hyacinthine chimes!
The world seems far away! I think I will
Divest myself of life's complexities;
Seek out the corners where the nymphs are still
And bathe my spirit in clear pools of peace.

Huw Menai

MONMOUTHSHIRE
Utrique fidelis – 'Faithful to both'

Faithful to England and to Wales,
but more faithful to each than to both.
Here are two voices:
the Welsh lilt of those who speak no Welsh
and the relaxed and rural West Country burr.

A county of mountains, forests and rivers,
Severn and Wye, Monnow, Usk, and Ebbw,
Wentwood, Wyndcliff, Sugarloaf, and Blorenge,
sheep and cattle and corn and salmon.

A county of coal, and steel, and aluminium,
iron, sheets, girders, tubes, and cables,
nylon, brakes, brushes, chemicals, and engineering.

A contested land of castles, a Flanders or a Poland,
a Wild West through history of Celts and Romans,
Silures, Saxons, Welsh, Danes, and Normans,
the unspeakable border barons of the March,
Chartists, the Coalowners, and the Miners' Federation.

Regionalized within itself, a microcosm,
where twenty miles seem five hundred.
It drinks with England and prays with Wales.
It has English tolerance, or indifference,
and Welsh rugby-fervour.
When the sun shines in the Valleys it is oval.
A land of meadows, bluebell glades, and foxes,
coaltips, choirs, and picturesque ruins,
teachers, preachers, gamblers, horsemen,
Labour and Tory sheep with unorthodox shepherds,
and some who cherish the grievances of possible ancestors.

Ivor Waters

JOHNNY ONIONS

From door to door along the sullen streets
he carries onion-bunches in the rain.
His beret, three-day beard, and Breton tongue
do not commend him, and he knocks in vain.

Yet hopefully at every frowning door
he holds his golden bunches in the light,
a lost enchanter fumbling for a spell
to take him from the greyness of the night.

Will no one buy? The Breton knocks again,
now sleepily, like one who dimly sees
his home and friends, and hears there in the rain
the rap of sabots on St. Malo quays.

Ivor Waters

HENRY MORGAN'S MARCH ON PANAMA

Morgan's hair is matted,
His lips are cracked and dry,
His tawny beard is tangled
And his plumed hat hangs awry:
But his voice still booms like thunder
Through the steaming jungle glade
As he marches, bold as Lucifer,
Leading his gaunt brigade.

Twelve hundred famished buccaneers,
Bitten, blistered and bled,
A sweltering mob, accursed and flayed
By the fierce sun overhead:
Twelve hundred starving scarecrows
With hardly a crust to eat,
And only sips from festering pools
In that grim, monstrous heat.

Twelve hundred tortured musketeers
Creeping through clogging mud
Where the reek of rotting mangroves
Wakes havoc in their blood:
Twelve hundred worn-out wretches
Fevered and almost dead,
But Morgan's fiery eloquence
Rallies them on ahead.

Twelve hundred tatterdemalions,
The sorriest, maddest crew
That ever the green savannahs saw
When the Spanish bugles blew:
Twelve hundred struggling skeletons
Who sprang to life and then
In one wild wave took Panama,
For they were Morgan's men.

A.G.Prys-Jones

THE REMEMBRANCE OF THE BARD

In the darkness of old age let not my memory fail:
Let me not forget to celebrate the beloved land of Gwent.
If they imprison me in a deep place, in a house of pestilence,
Still shall I be free, remembering the sunshine upon
  Mynydd Maen.
There have I listened to the song of the lark, my soul has
  ascended with the song of the little bird:
The great white clouds were the ships of my spirit, sailing to
  the haven of the Almighty.
Equally to be held in honour is the site of the Great
  Mountain.
Adorned with the gushing of many waters—sweet is the
  shade of its hazel thickets.
There a treasure is preserved which I will not celebrate;
It is glorious and deeply concealed.
If Teilo should return, if happiness were restored to the
  Cymri,
Dewi and Dyfrig should serve his Mass; then a great marvel
  would be made visible.
O blessed and miraculous work! then should my bliss be as
  the joy of angels.
I had rather behold this offering than kiss the twin lips of
  dark Gwenllian.
Dear my land of Gwent: *O quam dilecta tabernacula.*
The rivers are like precious golden streams of Paradise, thy
  hills are as the Mount Syon.
Better a grave on Twyn Bwrlwm than a throne in the palace
  of the Saxons at Caer-Ludd.

Arthur Machen

GWRANDO ARNA'I, ARGLWYDD GRIST

Gwrando arna'i, Arglwydd Grist, rwy i yn drist ofnadwy,
Am na bawn i, yn ddiwad, ynghenol gwlad Sir Fynwy.
Ar hyd Gwynedd odwi'n awr yn rhodio clawr ei brynie,
Gwell genny', myn Dduw, fy mod yn trigo yn Sir Fynwy.

Er y cerddes ym mhob sir, mi ddweta wir a'm geni,
Nad oes neb n'un lle i'w gael, fel pobl hael Sir Fynwy.
Ydwy'n hysbys ym mhob man, mewn llys a llan a phentre,
Ond ni weles debyg gwŷr i haelion pur Sir Fynwy.

Mi wn nad oes (Duw dy nawdd) un wlad mor hardd yn
   unlle,
I ddyn tlawd gael modd i fyw, a bendith, na Sir Fynwy,
Gan mor ffrwythlon yw'r wlad hon, mae'r Iesu Gwyn, heb
   ame,
Yn rho'i fendith ddydd a nos i aros yn Sir Fynwy.

Anonymous

LISTEN TO ME, LORD CHRIST

Listen to me, Lord Christ, I am dreadfully sad,
Because, rejected, I am not in the midst of the land of
   Monmouthshire.
Throughout Gwynedd I am now walking the surface of its
   hills,
I would rather, by God, be living in Monmouthshire.

Though I have walked in every shire, I tell you truly by my
   birth,
That there is no one anywhere to match the generous folk
   of Monmouthshire.
I am known everywhere, at court and church and village,
But I have never seen men as purely generous as those of
   Monmouthshire.

I know (may God protect me) there is nowhere a land so
   agreeable,
For a poor man to earn sustenance and a blessing than in
   Monmouthshire.
Since this land is so fruitful, the blessed Jesus, without
   doubt,
Gives his blessing day and night to rest on Monmouthshire.

                                        Translated by the Editor

ROADS

I love roads:
The goddesses that dwell
Far along invisible
Are my favourite gods.

Roads go on
While we forget, and are
Forgotten like a star
That shoots and is gone.

On this earth 'tis sure
We men have not made
Anything that doth fade
So soon, so long endure:

The hill road wet with rain
In the sun would not gleam
Like a winding stream
If we trod it not again.

They are lonely
While we sleep, lonelier
For lack of the traveller
Who is now a dream only.

From dawn's twilight
And all the clouds like sheep
On the mountains of sleep
They wind into the night.

The next turn may reveal
Heaven: upon the crest
The close pine clump, at rest
And black, may Hell conceal.

Often footsore, never
Yet of the road I weary,
Though long and steep and dreary,
As it winds on for ever.

Helen of the roads,
The mountain ways of Wales
And the Mabinogion tales
Is one of the true gods,

Abiding in the trees,
The threes and fours so wise,
The larger companies,
That by the roadside be,

And beneath the rafter
Else uninhabited
Excepting by the dead;
And it is her laughter

At morn and night I hear
When the thrush cock sings
Bright irrelevant things,
And when the chanticleer

Calls back to their own night
Troops that make loneliness
With their light footsteps' press,
As Helen's own are light.

Now all roads lead to France
And heavy is the tread
Of the living; but the dead
Returning lightly dance:

Whatever the road bring
To me or take from me,
They keep me company
With their pattering,

Crowding the solitude
Of the loops over the downs,
Hushing the roar of towns
And their brief multitude.

Edward Thomas

NOTES TO THE POEMS

Idris Davies: **I was born in Rhymney** (Extract) p. 17

This extract is the opening sequence of Idris Davies's auto-biographical poem 'I was born in Rhymney', completed 1943.

l. 15, Spurgeon: Charles Haddon Spurgeon (1834-1892), the famous Calvinist preacher.

l. 48, D.L.G.: David Lloyd George, as Liberal Chancellor of the Exchequer (1908-1915), introduced such social reforms as old age pensions and national insurance. He served in the Cabinet during the First World War and as Prime Minister from 1916 to 1922.

l. 61, I lost my native language: This was not literally true but it suits Idris Davies's poetic purposes to claim he lost his Welsh at school.

Idris Davies: **Cwmsyfiog** p. 25

Idris Davies taught at Cwmsyfiog School, five miles from Rhymney.

Idris Davies: **The Sacred Road** p. 28

The poem is Idris Davies's response to the Chartist march on Newport in November 1839.

Idris Davies: **Monmouthshire** p. 29

The identity of Monmouth was complicated by its subjection to the courts of Westminster, while ecclesiastically it remained part of the diocese of Llandaf. This separation was the main factor in references to 'Wales and Monmouthshire' in Acts of Parliament after 1536. Idris Davies is in no doubt as to the Welsh identity of Monmouthshire.

Idris Davies: **In the Places of My Boyhood** p. 30

l. 2, Some mining in the Rhymni Valley continued for many years. Idris Davies became a collier at the age of fourteen, working at a pit, where his father was a chief winder-man. In 1926 he lost a finger in a colliery accident.

Idris Davies: **In the Dusk** p. 33

l. 11, the Silurian: Gwent was a part of the territory of the Silures, the dominant Celtic tribe in South Wales.

Idris Davies: **O what can you give me?** p. 35

This powerful poem has been set to music. The poem is from Idris Davies's 1938 collection entitled *Gwalia Deserta*, which has as its theme the desert of industrial South Wales during the 1920s.

Idris Davies: **Cwm Rhymni** p. 36

One of Idris Davies's Welsh language poems. It was written in August 1945 and broadcast on radio in February 1946.

John Tripp: **In Memory of Idris Davies** p. 39

This poem establishes Idris Davies as a poet of a particular place – the Rhymni Valley. Glyn Jones, to whom the poem is dedicated, was one of Wales's leading writers of both poetry and prose.

l. 1, Silurians: In the nineteenth century it was argued that the Silures were Iberians, the pre-Celtic inhabitants of south-east Wales.

ll. 49–50, These lines refer to two of Idris Davies's poems – 'O what can you give me?' and 'Send out your homing pigeons, Dai'.

John Tripp: **Homage to Aneurin Bevan** p. 41

Aneurin Bevan was the Labour Member of Parliament for Ebbw Vale from 1929 to 1960.

Irene Thomas: **Memorial to Aneurin Bevan** p. 44

l. 5, Waun-y-Pound: A memorial honouring Aneurin Bevan was erected in 1972 on the Waun-y-Pound road above Tredegar. The three massive monoliths surrounding a central one represent Ebbw Vale, Tredegar and Rhymni.

l. 9, Strong medicine: The establishment of the National Health Service is regarded as Aneurin Bevan's greatest achievement.

Mick Morden: **Cawl** p. 45

Cawl is the Welsh for broth.

l. 4, Spitalfields: in London's East End, where the poet's mother was brought up.

Irene Thomas: **Coal Dust Grey** p. 47

The poem is from a collection entitled *Old Ebbw Vale in Poetry*.

l. 2, bailey: yard.

l. 3, spencers: jackets.

l. 4, Combinations: under-garments consisting of combined vest and pants.

l. 30, blue-bag: The blue-bag contained the product used in laundering to make clothes white by counteracting with blue colouring the tendency of clothes to become yellow.

Christopher Meredith: **Taking My Mother to Troed** p. 54

This is the fifth from the sequence 'Six Poems for Troedrhiwgwair', published in Christopher Meredith's 1990 collection entitled *Snaring Heaven*. Troedrhiwgwair, south-east of Tredegar, is in the Sirhowy Valley.

Christopher Meredith: **In Ebenezer Churchyard, Sirhowy** p. 55

l. 24, Jane Pryce late of Merioneth.

l. 39, *Cadernid ffydd*: the power of faith.

Harri Webb: **The Stars of Mexico** p. 62

The Chartist march to Newport took place on 3rd November, 1839. The speaker of this poem came from the Ebbw Vale and Nantyglo contingent led by Zephaniah Williams.

l. 13, the storm winds blew: The march took place on a very wet Sunday night.

l. 24, the Alamo: The site of the famous suicide stand by an American garrison against the Mexican army in 1836. The speaker of the poem could not have logically taken part in this particular stand, given the date of the Chartist march (1839). It is more likely that he took part in the 1846-1848 war between Mexico and the U.S.A.

Islwyn: **Tŷ'r Agent, Ynysddu** p. 63

Islwyn was born in Tŷ'r Agent, so called because his father was agent to the Llanarth family.

Graham Thomas: **At Ynysddu** p. 64

Ynysddu, one of the line of old colliery towns along the Sirhowy Valley, was the birthplace of Islwyn, one of the greatest Welsh poets of the nineteenth century.

l. 4, Cwmfelinfach: Islwyn is buried at Babell Church, Cwmfelin-fach, near Ynysddu. The place-name Cwmfelinfach means valley of the little mill.

Islwyn: **The Nightingale** p. 65

This is one of twenty-nine poems written by Islwyn in English and published in Hannah Williams and Tom Evans (1913) *Islwyn's English Poems*, Cardiff: The Educational Publishing Co. Ltd.

Islwyn: **The Storm** (Extract) p. 69

Islwyn wrote two long poems entitled 'Y Storm' ('The Storm') in 1854-1856 after the sudden death of his fiancée Anne Bowen. The anthologised extract is from the second poem.

l. 14, Jacob's well: a Biblical reference to John 1V, 6.

l. 28, Ida: In a cave on this mountain in Crete, Zeus is said to have been born.

Islwyn: **Joyous Multitude** p. 71

'Hapus Dyrfa' ('Joyous Multitude') is one of Islwyn's famous hymns.

Edmund Williams: **A Longing for Christ** p. 75

Some of Edmund Williams's hymns were published in 1741 in Pontypool by S. Mason. This particular hymn is from a 1742 collection, *Rhai Hymnau Duwiol* (Some Godly Hymns) published by Felix Farley of Bristol.

Anonymous: **Two Traditional Verses** p. 76

These two traditional verses are examples of the *triban*, a four-lined verse with seven syllables in the first, second and fourth lines and eight in the third. The first, second and fourth lines end with an unstressed syllable and are based on the same rhyme. L. 3 ends with a stressed syllable and rhymes with a word in the middle of the fourth line. Myfyr Wyn includes both verses in his *Atgofion am Sirhowy a'r Cylch* (Memories of Sirhowy and District).

l. 5, puddler: one who stirs about and turns over molten iron in a reverberatory furnace. The Sirhowy ironworks of 1778 were Gwent's first coke-fired blast furnaces.

l. 6, moulder: maker of moulds for casting.

Harri Webb: **From Risca with Love** p. 77

l. 4, paints the signposts green: a reference to the activities of the Welsh Language Society, formed in 1962. Society members painted out English roadsigns in many parts of Wales as a protest against the inferior legal status of the Welsh language.

l. 6, Monmouthshire became Gwent in 1974 with local government reorganisation.

Dafydd ap Gwilym: **Ifor the Generous** p. 79

Ifor Hael (Ifor the Generous) to whom the poem is addressed was Ifor ap Llewelyn of Bassaleg, a patron of the poet. Dafydd ap Gwilym's poem is an example of the *cywydd*, one of the major metrical forms in Welsh and Dafydd's favourite verse form. The cywydd consists of rhyming couplets with seven syllables in each line. It employs *cynghanedd* with an alternate stress on the penultimate or final syllable of each line.

l. 8, bragget: a drink of honey and ale.

l. 10, Rhydderch: one of the legendary 'Three Generous Men'.

Ieuan Brydydd Hir: **To the Hall of Ifor the Generous** p. 83

The ruins of Ifor's house at Gwernyclepa near Bassaleg inspired Ieuan Brydydd Hir (Evan Evans) to write his famous sequence of *englynion*. The *englyn*, the oldest recorded Welsh metrical form, is normally made up of four lines with *cynghanedd* and a single rhyme.

196

Crwys: **Bassaleg** p. 84

Maesaleg is the Welsh form for Bassaleg. Crwys's poem makes reference to Dafydd ap Gwilym and to Ieuan Brydydd Hir's *englynion*.

l. 12, Morfudd: Many of Dafydd ap Gwilym's *cywyddau* were addressed to Morfudd, his most cherished sweetheart.

Gillian Clarke: **From Clarence Bridge, Newport** p. 87

l. 1, Esk. Isca: the Brythoneg and Latin forms for the river Usk.

W.J.Gruffydd: **Cefn Mably** p. 89

Cefn Mably, near Castleton and once the home of the Kemeys family, is just inside the county boundary. Cefn Mably commemorates Mabel, the daughter of Robert Fitzhamon, the Norman conqueror of Glamorgan. Mabel built the original twelfth-century house. The Kemeys family acquired the house in the fifteenth century.

W.H.Davies: **Days that have been** p. 92

l. 15, Llantarnam and Malpas are situated between Cwmbran and W.H.Davies's native town, Newport. In his prose work *A Poet's Pilgrimage* (1918) W.H.Davies describes one of the local inns at Llantarnum (sic), called to this day 'The Three Blackbirds'. The ancient village of Magor lies between Newport and Chepstow. Llanwern, situated between Newport and Magor, has been since 1962 the site of the famous steelworks.

l. 16, Liswery is a southern district of Newport and Alteryn is in the north-western part of the town. W.H.Davies's spelling of "Alteryn" reflects the local pronunciation and is a corruption of the Welsh, Allt-yr-Ynn, i.e. Ash trees wood (or possibly hill).In *A Poet's Pilgrimage* (1918), page 201 Davies refers to Alteryn as 'the most beautiful part of Newport'.

The Roman remains, in particular, account for the description of 'Old Caerleon'.

W.H.Davies: **The Child and the Mariner** (Extract) p. 93

The child referred to in the title is W.H.Davies and the mariner is the poet's grandfather, a retired sea captain. W.H.Davies's grandfather kept the Church House Inn in Pill, Newport, where the poet spent his formative years. The first chapter of W.H.Davies's famous autobiography, *The Autobiography of a Supertramp*, has some memorable descriptions of Captain Davies.

Colin Palfrey: **Twm Barlwm** p. 98

Twyn Barlwm (Barlwm's Mound) is the mountain between Risca and Cwmbran. Barlwm was a local chieftain said to be buried here. The mountain is popularly known as Twm Barlwm.

Myfanwy Haycock: **The Canal near Pontypool** p. 100

The original Monmouthshire Canal was completed in 1796 and stretched from Pontnewynydd (where Myfanwy Haycock was born) to Newport. A branch to Crumlin was opened shortly after and in 1797 the Brecknock and Abergavenny Canal was begun, which extended the Pontypool branch as far as Brecon. There is no hint in this poem of the canal's original industrial function – to carry coal and iron to Newport docks.

John Barnie: **The Town where I was born** p. 104

John Barnie was brought up in Abergavenny during the 1940s and 1950s.

l. 11, the Blorenge: the hill to the south west of Abergavenny situated between the town and industrial Blaenafon.

Mark Harrell: **Summerhome (iii)** p. 107

l. 11, 'Deheubarth': With Gwynedd and Powys, Deheubarth was one of the three Kingdoms of Wales in the twelfth century.

Trefin: **The Abergavenny Murders** p. 109

The poem relates the treachery of the Norman William de Braose in 1175 at Abergavenny. De Braose, one of the twelfth-century Norman rulers of the castle strongholds in Gwent, is often regarded as the greatest blackguard in Welsh history. At Christmas time in 1175 de Braose invited the Welsh chieftains of Gwent Uwchcoed, among them Seisyll ap Dyfnwal, to a feast in Abergavenny castle, which was under Norman control at the time. De Braose had all the chieftains massacred: only Iorwerth of Caerleon escaped. Raymond Williams has a fascinating version of the story, entitled 'The Abergavenny Murders', in the second volume of his *People of the Black Mountains: The Eggs of the Eagle*.

Guto'r Glyn: **In Praise of Coldbrook, Sir Richard Herbert's Mansion** p. 113

Sir Richard Herbert was a brother of William Herbert, Earl of Pembroke. Both brothers were executed by the Lancastrians after the defeat of the Yorkists at Edgecote in 1469. Guto'r Glyn addressed many poems to the Herbert family. Coldbrook is situated some two miles south of Abergavenny. In 1891 Coldbrook went back to the Herberts, when it was purchased by Lady Llanofer.

l. 6, Einion Yrth: one of the eight sons of Cunedda, the fifth-century chieftain of the Gododdin tribe. The eight sons are each said to have established a dynasty in Wales.

l. 11, An ancient philosopher: Diogenes, the Greek philosopher of the Cynic sect, who praised self-sufficiency and despised social conventions.

l. 12, a tub: Diogenes chose to live in a tub.

l. 15-16, Diogenes is said to have asked Alexander the Great not to stand between him and the sun.

l. 22, Virgil: Virgil had acquired a reputation as a magician by the Middle Ages. It was widely believed that Virgil had built a castle for the emperor from which everything that was happening in Rome could be seen and heard.

l. 26, St Paul's: Its clock tower was the highest in Europe (before 1561, when it was struck by lightning).

l. 27, His two magnificent houses: A second Coldbrook mansion was situated at Llandenny near Raglan.

l. 29, Ehangwen: King Arthur's hall is referred to as Ehangwen in the tale of Culhwch and Olwen in the *Mabinogion*.

l. 59, The three cantrefs: Gwent Uwchcoed and Gwent Iscoed are the two cantrefs of Gwent. There is, however, reference to a third cantref in many old Welsh manuscripts.

l. 64, There is a legend that Noah was commanded to hang up the true and genuine philosopher's stone in the ark, to give light to every living creature within.

Trefin: **Llanofer Hall** p. 119

Llanofer Hall, now on the A4042 Abergavenny to Pontypool road, was the home of Lord and Lady Llanofer. Lady Llanofer (1802-1896) in particular was a patron of Welsh culture; her husband, Benjamin Hall, Lord Llanofer, gave his name to the famous clock, Big Ben, in the Houses of Parliament.

l. 9, Fine books: The Llanofer manuscripts included several Welsh medieval prose texts; a unique Welsh translation of *Gesta Romanorum*; the papers of the famous poet and scholar, Iolo Morgannwg; and documents on the Cymreigyddion society of Abergavenny.

l. 13, Gwenynen Gwent: Lady Llanofer's bardic name – lit. the Bee of Gwent.

Anthony Howell: **Border Country** (Extract) p. 126

The poem, which describes a car journey through border country, was composed as part of the Hay on Wye Festival of Literature in 1990.

l. 9, Llanthony: In the north-west of Gwent just across the border between Wales and England. The name is a corruption of Llanddewi Nant Honddu – the church of St. David on the Honddu brook.

l. 13, Cymyoy: a few miles north of Llanthony.

l. 14, Its tower askew: The valley side is subject to landslips and subsidence. The church walls and tower have been affected.

l. 52, Lord Hereford's – the Tumpa: Lord Hereford's Knob or Twmpa, a few miles south of Hay on Wye.

l. 64, Gospel Pass: to the east of Lord Hereford's Knob.

l. 70, the book shop town: Hay has over twenty second-hand bookshops.

Walter Savage Landor: **Fiesolan Musings** (Extract) p. 129

The poet, Walter Savage Landor, bought Llanthony Abbey in 1808 for £20,000, fully intending to restore the ruins and establish an ideal community. By 1813 a disillusioned Landor had left for Swansea, harassed by lawsuits and debts. The title of the poem refers to Fiesole above Florence, where Landor had a villa from 1829.

ll. 3-6, These lines refer to the improvements Landor had introduced on his Llanthony estate. The sheep, the hardy Merino, were imported from Spain.

l. 18, *Morning Post*: the oldest London daily newspaper.

John Tripp: **A David Jones Mural at Llanthony** p. 131

David Jones (1895 -1974) was both writer and artist. In the 1920s David Jones was a member of Eric Gill's Catholic community of craftsmen and artists at Capel-y-Ffin. The poem is dedicated to Jeremy Hooker who has written extensively on the work of David Jones.

l. 35, Flanders: David Jones served as a private with the Royal Welch Fusiliers during the First World War.

l. 37, sanity: In 1933 David Jones suffered the first of his many breakdowns in health.

l. 48, Harrow: David Jones lived in Harrow-on-the-Hill.

Thomas Churchyard: **The Worthines of Wales** (Extract) p. 135

Thomas Churchyard's long poem was first written in 1587. This extract comes from a section of the poem entitled 'The Castles and Townes neere Oske, and there aboutes'. The original orthography has been retained to give readers some sense of Churchyard's Elizabethan English.

l. 18, Thomas Churchyard notes that 'King Edward the fourth and his children (as some affirme), and King Richard the third, were borne here'. So far as I am aware, there is no historical evidence to support these details.

l. 33, Three castles: the so-called trilateral castles of Grosmont, Skenfrith and White Castle.

l. 42, Langibby: Probably Castell Tregrug is meant here. The castle was built about 1300 by Gilbert de Clare, the last Earl of Gloucester. It was never properly finished, but it had one of the biggest inner wards in Wales.

l. 54, King Arthur's golden Hall: Arthur, it is rumoured, had his court in Caerleon on the grassy mound which in Churchyard's day covered the Roman Amphitheatre and which was known as King Arthur's Round Table. One legend says King Arthur caught salmon from the River Usk to serve at his Round Table!

Catherine Fisher: **Poem for David Lewis** p. 138

David Lewis (1617-1679) was born of a Catholic mother in Abergavenny. He converted to Roman Catholicism in 1630 and was ordained priest in 1642. He ministered to many Catholic families in South Wales, particularly to the Morgans of Llantarnam. He was known as '*Tad y Tlodion*' (Father of the Poor). David Lewis was arrested on his way to mass on the orders of John Arnold of Llanfihangel Crucorney, the local Member of Parliament and a fanatical opponent of Catholicism. David Lewis was canonized in 1970 as one of the Forty Martyrs of England and Wales.

l. 4, The official hangman refused to carry out the execution.

Dafydd Benwyn: **Sir William and Lady Powell** (Extract) p. 140

Sir William Powell was knighted by King James I. Lady Powell was the daughter of Sir Thomas Morgan of Pencoed near Penhow and sister to Sir William Morgan.

ll. 7-8, Sir William's father was a certain Dafydd Philip to whom Dafydd Benwyn addressed a funeral elegy.

ll. 15-17, As already noted, Lady Powell was the daughter of Sir Thomas Morgan of Pencoed and sister to Sir William Morgan, also of Pencoed. Sir Thomas was the son of Sir William Morgan and grandson of Sir Thomas Morgan, so that the claim that the lady was the grandchild of two knights, the great-grandchild of another knight and sister to yet another knight is perfectly accurate.

Lewys Glyn Cothi: **Ode in Praise of Trahaearn** (Extract) p. 143

Trahaearn ap Ieuan, Lord of Penrhos near Caerleon, was Steward of Caerleon in 1454.

l. 10 ,Rhirid Flaidd: Lord of Penllyn in Meirionnydd.

l. 16, The reference is to the coats of arms of Adam ap Iorwerth and Rhirid Flaidd.

l. 19, Fwrdios: Bwrdios is the Welsh for Bordeaux, famous for its claret. The poet is praising the hospitality of Penrhos.

Clifford Dyment: **Derbyshire Born, Monmouth is My Home** p. 144

l. 15, Brachets: hounds.

l. 38, Christy minstrels: minstrels who imitated Negroes, originated by a certain George Christy of New York.

Catherine Fisher: **Frosty Morning, Caerleon** p. 146

This poem is the second in a series of four Archaeology Poems included in Catherine Fisher's collection entitled *Immrama* (an old Irish word meaning 'voyages to islands').

l. 10, Barracks: remains of Roman barracks in Caerleon.

l. 11, amphitheatre: built just outside the fortress defences of Caerleon about 80 A.D.

A.G.Prys-Jones: **To Valeria** p. 148

l. 17, oleander: an evergreen shrub.

l. 42, seisin: possession.

l. 44, Tyrrhenian sea: the part of the Mediterranean between the Italian mainland and Corsica, Sardinia and Sicily.

Dafydd Llwyd: **To William Herbert** p. 151

William Herbert, Earl of Pembroke, was the founder of the famous Herbert clan and the leading Welsh supporter of the Yorkists in the Wars of the Roses. He was the son of William ap Thomas of Raglan and Gwladys, the daughter of Dafydd Gam. The poets regarded William Herbert as the quintessential Welsh hero.

l. 33, Vortemir: the son of Vortigern, the king of the Britons in the fifth century. Vortigern invited the Saxons to Britain to withstand the raids by the Picts and the Scots. The plan rebounded on Vortigern, when the Saxons turned against him and seized lands in Kent, killing his son Vortemir.

l. 34, the deed done to Llywelyn: On 11th December, 1282, Llywelyn was killed by English troops at a bridge over the Irfon, near Builth.

l. 38, The swallow's fledgling: the young Henry Tudor, who came under William Herbert's care, when the latter captured the Lancastrian stronghold of Pembroke.

l. 39, In his will William Herbert arranged the engagement of his daughter, Maud, to Henry Tudor.

l. 43, Cadwgan: a Welsh prince of the late eleventh and early twelfth centuries.

Alfred, Lord Tennyson: **The Hushing of the Wye** p. 156

Tennyson wrote this section of his memorial sequence 'In Memoriam' at Tintern Abbey on the Wye. He was struck by the high tide pushing up from the Severn, how 'the rapids of the Wye are stilled by the incoming sea'.

Ivor Waters: **Mudding** p. 157

The Wye is tidal in its lower reaches.

l. 14, Old Moore: Old Moore's Almanack as a calendar of the year offers information about tides.

l. 31, Flooding: Great floods have occurred every five hundred years or so. There was one in 430, in 1095 and most dramatically of all in 1606. A stone marking the height of the 1606 flood is to be seen in a wall by the door of Redwick Church.

Robert Bloomfield: **The Banks of Wye** (Extract) p. 158

Taken from Book 2 of Robert Bloomfield's 'The Banks of Wye; a Poem in Four Books'.

l. 2, Ships were once built in Llandogo, when it was a thriving river-port. There was a shuttle sevice of sailing ships, conveying goods and passengers between the lower Wye valley and Bristol.

William Wordsworth: **Lines Written a Few Miles above Tintern Abbey** p. 159

In the first edition of *Lyrical Ballads and Poems* (1798) the full title appears as 'Lines composed a few miles above Tintern Abbey, on revisiting the banks of the Wye during a tour'.

l. 1, Five years have passed: Wordsworth visited the Wye in 1793 and again in 1798.

l. 4, inland murmur: Wordsworth noted that 'The river is not affected by the tides a few miles above Tintern'.

l. 60, Thou wanderer: The Latin form for the Wye is Vaga, meaning vagrant.

l. 120, my dearest friend: Wordsworth was accompanied by his sister Dorothy on the second tour of the Wye.

Alun: **Abaty Tintern** p. 165

Alun's poem is an adaptation of an English poem – apart from the rather weak last four lines.

Edward Davies: **Chepstow: The Castle** (Extract) p. 167

This is an extract from the second canto of Edward Davies's long poem 'Chepstow: A Poem in Five Cantos', first published in 1784.

l. 8, ivy bush: supposed to be the largest in the country.

l. 19, Harry Marten: Henry Marten (1602-1680) was one of the signatories to the death warrant of Charles 1, hence the label 'the Regicide'. At the Restoration he was imprisoned in Chepstow Castle.

l. 29, died: Henry Marten died in prison.

l. 40, old Baucis and Philemon: the poetical names of the former governor and governess of Chepstow Castle.

Edward Davies: **Chepstow: The Bridge** (Extract) p. 169

This is an extract from the third canto of the poem. The bridge over the River Wye linked Monmouthshire and Gloucestershire.

Catherine Fisher: **St. Tewdric's Well** p. 170

The place-name Mathern, near Chepstow, derives from Merthyr Tewdric (Tewdric's burial place). Tewdric, a sixth / seventh-century ruler of Gwent, relinquished his power to his son Meyric, to become a holy recluse. An unexpected Saxon invasion, however, made Tewdric return to lead his people into battle on the banks of the Wye. Meyric's army was victorious but Tewdric was wounded and died three days later at Mathern. From the spot where he died sprang a fountain of clear water, which became known as St. Tewdric's Well. The story is recorded on a tablet on the north wall of the chancel at Mathern parish church.

l. 16, Bran: Brân was father of the Welsh king Caradog who fought against the Roman invaders. Some claim that Brân is buried at Cwmbran which was named after him.

Alison Bielski: **well at Trellech** p. 171

The so-called Virtuous Well is situated in a field to the south-east of the village of Trellech. Its water is thought to have healing properties.

Alison Bielski: **invaders** p. 172

l. 3 ,Hell: the Severn tunnel.

l. 7, Julius Frontinus: the Roman governor who established the fortress of Isca Silurum (Caerleon).

l. 14, Wentwood's twin peaks: the once dense forest which divided Gwent Uwchcoed (Gwent above the wood) and Gwent Iscoed (Gwent below the wood).

l. 20, Harold's intruding palace: Harold Godwinson (killed at the Battle of Hastings in 1066) attempted to claim Gwent Iscoed for his earldom of Hereford in 1065. It is thought that he ordered the construction of a manorial court at Portskewett (Porthiscoed). Caradog ap Gruffudd demolished the building, killing Harold's servants.

l. 21, Black Pagans: the Vikings.

Peter Finch: **Severn Estuary ABC** p. 175
Peter Finch has commented that 'For much of the post-war period the area had a higher density of [nuclear] reactors than anywhere else in Europe'.

Catherine Fisher: **Severn Bore** p. 176
l. 6, a king: Edward 11 was murdered in Berkeley Castle.

l. 11, Ivor Gurney's ghost: Ivor Gurney, the poet and composer, was born at Gloucester in 1890 and died in 1937. His first collection of poems, *Severn and Somme*, was published in 1917.

l. 21, the town: Gloucester.

Frances Homfray: **Thoughts on Happiness** (Extract) p. 177
l. 26, Striguil: In Norman times, and for centuries later, Chepstow was named Striguil.

Huw Menai: **In Monmouthshire** (To W.J.T.C.) p. 182
This poem, published during the Second World War, was dedicated to William John Townsend Collins (1868-1952), editor of the *South Wales Argus* newspaper from 1917 to 1939.

Ivor Waters: **Monmouthshire** p. 184
l. 20, It drinks with England: Many parts of Wales were 'dry' on Sundays.

A.G.Prys-Jones: **Henry Morgan's March on Panama** p. 186
There is much confusion over the birthplace of Henry Morgan (1635?-1688), the famous buccaneer. Some claim Morgan was born at Llangattock Lingoed, a hamlet some seven miles north east of Abergavenny. Other sources assert that Henry Morgan was born on a mountain farm on the banks of the Rhymney river, near Tredegar.

Nor is it improbable that Morgan was born at Tredegar House near Newport, the ancestral seat of the Morgans, the rich gentry family to whom he belonged. In 1658 Henry Morgan went to Barbados as an indentured labourer, where he worked for four years. He became a pirate and later a privateer in the Caribbean. This poem describes one of Morgan's exploits against the Spaniards in the service of Jamaica's Governor. The march on Panama took place in 1671. Morgan was knighted by Charles 11 in 1674 and made Deputy-Governor of Jamaica.

Anonymous: **Listen to me, Lord Christ** p. 189

This anonymous tribute to Monmouthshire was found in a Welsh manuscript scrapbook dating from Elizabeth 1's reign. It was first published by John Hobson Matthews in an article entitled 'Old Monmouth' in *Archaeologia Cambrensis, Vol. 1X*, 1909, pp.15 -34.

Arthur Machen: **The Remembrance of the Bard** p. 187

l. 15, *O quam dilecta tabernacula*: An echo of the opening of Psalm 84 which begins with 'How amiable are thy tabernacles!'

Edward Thomas: **Roads** p. 190

l. 33, Helen of the roads: Helen is from *The Mabinogion*, the collection of Welsh tales. In the tale 'The Dream of Macsen Wledig', Helen is married to Macsen the Emperor. She gave her name to the great old mountain road known as Sarn Helen. In the tale Macsen gave Helen three castles – one in North Wales at Arfon, one at Caerleon and one at Carmarthen. It was Helen's idea to have roads linking the three castles.

l. 36, one of the true gods: Helen, according to mythologists, is one of the travelling goddesses of the dusk. Edward Thomas's wife was also named Helen.

l. 53, Now all roads lead to France: The poem was written during the First World War. Edward Thomas enlisted in July 1915 and was killed at the Battle of Arras in April 1917.

BIOGRAPHICAL NOTES

SAM ADAMS: born 1934 at Gilfach Goch in Glamorgan. Formerly an English lecturer at Caerleon College of Education, thereafter HMI. His collection of poems *The Boy Inside* was published in 1973.

ALUN (1797-1840): bardic name of John Blackwell, who was born near Mold in Flintshire. Entered Jesus College, Oxford in 1824 and ordained curate at Holywell five years later. Remembered today for his lyric poetry.

JOHN BARNIE: born 1941 in Abergavenny. Taught at the University of Copenhagen. Editor of *Planet* magazine. Recent publications include *Heroes* (1996) and *The Wine Bird* (1998).

ALISON BIELSKI: born 1925 in Newport. Has published books on local folklore as well as many collections of poetry, which include *Across the Burning Sand*, *Mermaid Poems*, *Night Sequence* and *Eagles*.

ROBERT BLOOMFIELD (1766-1823): born in Suffolk and worked as a farm labourer and shoemaker. Undertook a journey in 1807 from Ross to Chepstow, from Raglan to Brecon and back through Hay and Hereford. Responded enthusiastically to the Monmouthshire landscape, likening its hills to the Alps.

THOMAS CHURCHYARD (c1520-1604): a native of Shrewsbury. Lived a wandering life partly as a soldier and partly as a hanger-on of the court and nobility. His topographical morality in verse, 'The Worthines of Wales' (1587) describes a journey to Monmouthshire and Breconshire, back to Ludlow and Shrewsbury, then north to Denbighshire and Flintshire.

GILLIAN CLARKE: born 1937 in Cardiff. Well known for her teaching of creative writing. Formerly editor of *The Anglo-Welsh Review*. Her *Collected Poems* appeared in 1997 and *Five Fields* in 1998.

W.J.T.COLLINS (1868-1952): editor of the *South Wales Argus* newspaper from 1917 to 1939. Well known for his coverage of rugby. Wrote two volumes of literary biography on Monmouthshire Writers as well as poetry and prose romances.

CRWYS (1875-1968): bardic name of William Crwys Williams. Born at Craig-cefn-Parc in Glamorgan. Spent many years as a Congregational minister at Rehoboth in Brynmawr. His shorter lyrics are among the best-known in the Welsh language.

DAFYDD AP GWILYM (c1320-1370): regarded as one of the greatest Welsh poets of all time. Probably born at Brogynin in the parish of Llanbadarn Fawr. Buried reputedly at Ystrad Fflur (Strata Florida).

DAFYDD BENWYN (fl 1550-1600): native of Llangeinor in Glamorgan. Addressed poems to the landed families of Gwent (the Morgans in particular) and Glamorgan. A selection of his poems was published by J.Kyrle Fletcher in *The Gwentian Poems of Dafydd Benwyn* (1909).

DAFYDD LLWYD (c1420-1500): native of Mathafarn. Prolific writer of *cywyddau*. A supporter of the Lancastrian side during the Wars of the Roses, yet wrote in praise of William Herbert, Earl of Pembroke, whom he saw as the deliverer of the Welsh.

EDWARD DAVIES (1718-1789): born at Llandaf. Vicar of Mathern and rector of Portskewett and later of Sudbrook. His work *Chepstow: a Poem in five Cantos* was published in 1794.

IDRIS DAVIES (1905-1953): born and bred in Rhymni. Lost a finger in a colliery accident in 1926. Qualified as a teacher. Published *Gwalia Deserta* (1938), *The Angry Summer* (1943) and *Tonypandy and Other Poems* (1945). Died of cancer in 1953.

W.H.DAVIES (1871-1940): born in Newport and brought up in the Church House Inn in Newport's dockland. In 1893 began six years of tramping back and forth over America, injuring himself in Ontario in 1899, as he attempted to jump a moving train. The famous *Autobiography of a Super-Tramp* appeared in 1908. *The Poems of W.H.Davies* was published in 1940.

CLIFFORD DYMENT (1914-1970): born Alfreton in Derbyshire but spent many years in Caerleon. *The Railway Game* (1962), his autobiography, illustrates his strong sense of Welsh identity. *Collected Poems* appeared in 1970.

EIDDIL GWENT (1798-1878): bardic name of David Morris. Spent most of his life in Tredegar working as a cobbler. Prominent member of Cymreigyddion y Fenni. His ballad 'Can Mlynedd i Nawr' (A Hundred Years from Now) is still read today.

PETER FINCH: born in Cardiff in 1947. Writer of much experimental poetry. Founder of magazine *Second Aeon* in 1966.

CATHERINE FISHER: born in Newport in 1956. Poet and children's novelist. *Immrama*, a first collection of poems, was published in 1988.

GUTO'R GLYN (c1435-1493): associated with Glyn Ceiriog in Denbighshire. Some of his verse reflects his military career on the Yorkist side in the Wars of the the Roses. Many poems are addressed to the Yorkist leader, William Herbert, the Earl of Pembroke. Regarded as second only to Dafydd ap Gwilym among the so-called Poets of the Gentry.

W.J.GRUFFYDD (1881-1954): born at Bethel in the parish of Llanddeiniolen, Caernarvonshire. Educated Jesus College, Oxford, where he read Classics and English Literature. Professor of Welsh at University College, Cardiff. Distinguished scholar and critic and an accomplished lyric poet. Lifelong interest in the National Eisteddfod.

GWENTWYSON (fl 1875): bardic name of Ezekiel Davies. Native of Sirhowy and mentioned in Myfyr Wyn's *Atgofion am Sirhowy a'r Cylch* (Memories of Sirhowy and District). Blacksmith by trade. Poet and musician. His undated *Ceinion Gwent* (Gems of Gwent) was published by E.Rees at Ystalyfera.

MARK HARRELL: born 1966 in Singapore. Has lived near Abergavenny for over twenty years. Educated Exeter and London Universities. Has a hitherto unpublished sequence of Gerald of Wales monologues entitled 'The Journey through Wales'.

MYFANWY HAYCOCK (1913-1963): born in Pontnewynydd near Pontypool. Artist and poet. Frequent broadcaster. Her volumes of poetry include: *Fantasy and Other Poems* (1937); *Poems* (1944); *More Poems* (1945).

FRANCIS HOMFRAY (fl 1817): rector of Llanfair Cilgedyn. His *Thoughts on Happiness* was published in 1817.

ANTHONY HOWELL: born 1945 in London. Novelist and poet.

IEUAN BRYDYDD HIR (c. 1733-1788): bardic name of Evan Evans. Born in Lledrod, Cardiganshire. Studied Merton College, Oxford. Curate in many Welsh and English parishes, including Bassaleg. Scholar and poet.

IOAN EMLYN (1820-1873): bardic name of John Emlyn Jones. Baptist minister and pastor with Nebo, Ebbw Vale from 1853 to 1861. Returned to Nebo in 1873 and was buried there. Closely connected to Cymreigyddion y Fenni. His fame rests on the simple lyric '*Bedd y Dyn Tylawd*' (The Pauper's Grave).

ISLWYN (1832-1878): bardic name of William Thomas. Born near Ynysddu and educated in Tredegar, Newport and Cowbridge. While he was preparing for the ministry in Swansea, his fiancée, Anne Bowen, died and in response Islwyn wrote two long poems, both entitled '*Y Storm*' (The Storm). Ordained a minister in 1859, he never took charge of a church. Buried at Babell Church, Cwmfelinfach near Ynysddu, which now houses a museum dedicated to the poet.

EVAN JAMES (1809-1878): kept the Ancient Druid Inn in Argoed in the parish of Bedwellty. His bardic name was Ieuan ap Iago. Evan James wrote the words of the Welsh national anthem, while his son, James James, composed the music.

WALTER SAVAGE LANDOR (1775-1864) : born at Warwick. In 1808 purchased Llanthony Abbey and its estates, building himself a house looking down on the abbey and planting many fine trees which remain to this day. In 1813 Landor left Llanthony harassed by lawsuits and debts.

LEWYS GLYN COTHI (c1420-1489) : often regarded as one of the greatest Welsh poets of the fifteenth century. Probably took his bardic name from Glyn Cothi near Llanybydder, Carmarthenshire. Like Dafydd Llwyd, his support for the Lancastrian cause during the Wars of the Roses did not prevent him from writing poetry for Yorkist patrons. Genealogy was a particular interest of his.

ARTHUR MACHEN (18631947): born in Caerleon. Novelist, short story writer and essayist. His works include the classic horror novel *The Great God Pan* (1894); the novel *The Hill of Dreams* (1907), four of whose seven chapters are set in Gwent; and the short story *The Bowman* (1915).

HUW MENAI (1887-1961): born Huw Menai Williams at Caernarfon, the son of a miner. Became a miner himself in 1906, losing his job because of his political agitation. His mother tongue was Welsh but published four volumes of poetry in English.

CHRISTOPHER MEREDITH: born in Tredegar in 1954. Novelist and poet.

MICK MORDEN : born in Croydon in 1934. Educated Jesus College, Cambridge. Formerly Principal of Pontypool and Usk College.

OSSIAN GWENT (1839-1892) : bardic name of John Davies. Born in Cardigan but moved to Rhymney, where he learned the carpenter's craft. Published *Caniadau* (1873) and *Blodau Gwent* (1898).

COLIN PALFREY : born 1939 in Cardiff. Poet, novelist and playwright. Worked in adult and higher education in Gwent.

A.G.PRYS-JONES (1888-1987) : born in Denbigh. Became an H.M.I. In 1917 edited the first anthology of Anglo-Welsh poetry, entitled *Welsh Poets*. Published six volumes of poetry.

JENNY SULLIVAN: born 1944 in Cardiff. Has lived in Raglan since 1980. Poet, short story writer and children's novelist.

ALFRED TENNYSON (1809-1902): born in Somersby, Lincolnshire. Appointed Poet Laureate in 1850, when "In Memoriam" was also published. Visited Tintern Abbey. Stayed at the Hanbury Arms in Caerleon, while gathering material for the Arthurian legends of his "Idylls of the King" (1859).

EDWARD THOMAS (1878-1917): born at Lambeth, London. Both parents came from Monmouthshire, his father from Tredegar and his mother from Newport. Spent many childhood holidays with his Welsh relatives in Caerleon. Enlisted in 1915 and killed at Arras in 1917.

GRAHAM THOMAS: born in Abertyleri in 1944. Educated at University College of Wales, Aberystwyth. Schoolteacher. His first volume of poetry *The One Place* was published in 1983.

IRENE THOMAS: born in Ebbw Vale in 1930. Former art teacher and freelance artist. Frequent broadcaster. Poems reflect her Ebbw Vale upbringing.

TREFIN (1889-1962): bardic name of Edgar Phillips. Active in the National Eisteddfod, served as keeper of the Great Sword and as Archdruid. Married to Maxwell Fraser, the travel writer.

JOHN TRIPP (1927-1986): born in Bargoed, Glamorgan. Worked as a journalist in London, returning to Wales in 1969. Literary editor of *Planet* from 1973 to 1979. *Collected Poems* (1958-78) appeared in 1978.

THOMAS VAUGHAN (1621-1666): Henry Vaughan's twin brother. The most important hermetical philosopher of his day. Wrote most of his poems in Latin but some half a dozen are in English.

IVOR WATERS (1907-1991): born at Chepstow. Local historian. Honorary Curator of Chepstow Museum from 1948 to 1963. Owner of the Moss Rose Press. *Collected Verse* published in 1977.

HARRI WEBB (1920-1994): born in Swansea. Worked as a Librarian in Merthyr Tudful and Mountain Ash. Poet and ballad writer. His *Collected Poems* published posthumously in 1995.

EDMUND WILLIAMS (1717-1742): born at Cwmtyleri. Converted to Methodism by Howel Harris. One of the early hymn writers of eighteenth-century Methodism in Wales.

WILLIAM WORDSWORTH (1770-1850): born at Cockermouth, Cumbria. The most famous of the Romantic Poets. His second visit to Tintern Abey was with the poet's sister, Dorothy.

ACKNOWLEDGEMENTS

Acknowledgements are due to the following publishers, or individuals:

For the poems by Sam Adams to Christopher Davies Ltd.

For the poems by John Barnie, Alison Bielski and Idris Davies to Gomer Press.

For the translation by Joseph Clancy to Macmillan.

For the poem by Gillian Clarke from *Letter from a Far Country* (1982) to Carcanet Press.

For the poem by W.J.T.Collins to R.H.Johns Ltd.

For the poem by Crwys to James Davies a'i Gwmni.

For the poems by W.H.Davies to Jonathan Cape Ltd.

For the poem by Clifford Dyment to Martin Starkie for and on behalf of Irene Dyment.

For the poems by Peter Finch, Catherine Fisher, Christopher Meredith, Graham Thomas and John Tripp to Seren Books.

For the poem by W.J.Gruffydd to Llyfrau'r Dryw.

For the poems by Myfanwy Haycock to Miss Gwladys Haycock.

For the poem by Anthony Howell to Wood Wind Publications, Birmingham.

For the translation by John Gwilym Jones.

For the poem by Arthur Machen to the Estate of Arthur Machen

For the poems by Huw Menai to Chapman & Hall.

For the translation by Dyfnallt Morgan to Mrs Eleri Eirug Morgan.

For the poems by A.G.Prys-Jones to Christopher Davies Ltd.

For the poem by Edward Thomas to Oxford University Press.

For the poems by Irene Thomas to Starling Press, Risca and Kerin Publishers.

For the poems by Trefin to the Educational Publishing Co., Cardiff and Wrexham.

.

For the poems by Ivor Waters to Mrs Mercedes Waters.

For the poems by Harri Webb to Meic Stephens and Gomer Press.

The editor and publishers are grateful to the poets for permission to reproduce their work.

It was not possible to contact some publishers, since firms no longer exist.